This
Sandra Lee
semi-homemade®
grilling

book belongs to:

141 Blue Cheese and Bacon-Stuffed Burgers

87 Tangerine Teriyaki Ribs

179 Mexican Pizzas

214 Skillet Cherry Cobbler

230 Cowboy Cocktail

Meredith® Books Des Moines, Iowa

Copyright © 2006 Sandra Lee Semi-Homemade® First Edition All rights reserved. Printed in the USA.
Library of Congress Control Number 2005938778   ISBN: 978-0-696-23221-3
Published by Meredith® Books. Des Moines, Iowa.

sem·i·home·made

adj. **1:** a stress-free solution-based formula that provides savvy shortcuts and affordable, timesaving tips for overextended do-it-yourself homemakers **2:** a quick and easy equation wherein 70% ready-made convenience products are added to 30% fresh ingredients with creative personal style, allowing homemakers to take 100% of the credit for something that looks, feels, or tastes homemade **3:** a foolproof resource for having it all—and having the time to enjoy it **4:** a method created by Sandra Lee for home, garden, crafts, beauty, food, fashion, and entertaining wherein everything looks, tastes, and feels as if it was made from scratch.

Solution-based **E**nterprise that **M**otivates, **I**nspires, and **H**elps **O**rganize and **M**anage time, while **E**nriching **M**odern life by **A**dding **D**ependable shortcuts **E**very day.

dedication

To my Uncle Bill and Grandpa Paul
who were generous enough to let the girls in on the "boys" barbecue action.
–sl

special thanks

To the grilling greats—from Steven Raichlen to Bobby Flay—
many thanks for teaching us how glorious great grilling can be.

acknowledgments

With admiration and appreciation to my production and publishing team:
Jeff, Ed, Lisa, Pamela, Mark, Laurent, Robin, Linda, Sara, Jan, Mick, Jessica, Steve, Gina,
Jim, Jeff, Doug, Bob, Jack, and the entire Meredith Team.
Thank you for helping me create "girl meets grill!"

appreciation

To the following manufacturers and retailers for their generous product contributions:
Room with a View, Vietri, Love Plates, Crate & Barrel, Kitchen Aid,
Napa Style, F&S Fabrics, Silk Trading Company, Pacific Rim, Barbecues Galore, Richard (Rick) Wiseley,
Harley-Davidson and the California chapters of H. O. G.® (Rick McDermed, Homer Hall, Eric Oltmann,
Susan VanAbel, Jeff Hanley, and Bob and Laura Schultz).

Table of Contents

Chapter 1

Beef and Veal
20

Chapter 2

Poultry
52

Chapter 3

Pork and Lamb
82

Chapter 4

Fish and Seafood
108

Letter from Sandra

We all just want to have fun—and grilling is the way to do it! I grew up grilling, but I really became a fan in college. At the University of Wisconsin, tailgate parties were a part of campus life. We'd fire up the grill in the parking lot and load it with the best of game-day gourmet. Beer brats and kraut, smoky burgers towering with toppings, hot dogs smothered in chili and cheese all bring back memories of great times and great food.

Today, I grill every chance I get, both for myself and for my friends and family. It's a fast, healthy way to cook all types of food for all types of occasions. Whether you're like my sister, Kimber—a busy parent trying to get a nutritious meal on the table—or my brothers, John and Rich—fun-loving guys kicking back with friends—grilling is delicious and doable for both sexes!

Semi-Homemade® Grilling celebrates the casual side of cooking, a return to the simple pleasures of food, friends, and a festive environment. Summertime or wintertime, grilling is easy the Semi-Homemade® way. My 70/30 philosophy makes it simple: Start with 70% ready-made products, add 30% fresh ingredients, then take 100% of the credit for a meal that's fast and fabulous!

Grilling is more than a meal; it's culinary magic. Every recipe in this book is designed to travel, letting you bring the outdoors in … or the indoors out. The chapters are a culinary mix of yin and yang—rich, meaty burgers and thick, juicy steaks, balanced with tender chicken, pork, and light, luscious seafood. There are recipes for all reasons and all seasons—refreshing marinades and cool, chunky salsas for summers when we linger outdoors and robust sauces and hot, hearty toppings for cooler months when we burrow inside. Food comes alive with flavorful contrasts—sharp Dijon mustard with sweet maple syrup, tangy barbecue sauce with creamy Kahlúa®, garlic and mint, prosciutto and fig.

The dishes are as companionable as the ingredients. Every dish works with every other—meats, sides, and desserts mixing à la carte to make a menu of meals. Served in smaller portions, entrées double as appetizers. Add cocktails, and every meal's a party, whether you're feeding a few friends or entertaining a crowd.

The oldest form of cooking is as enticing as the flicker of a flame. That irresistible seared-in flavor, the relaxed ambiance, the cherished company of friends and loved ones all make grilling the secret ingredient to a great gathering. If you can cook it, you can grill it … the Semi-Homemade® way.

Cheers to healthy, happy grilling!

With a warm hug,

Sandra Lee

Outdoor Grilling

Outdoor cooking summons feel-good memories—happy thoughts of sun, sand, and carefree cookouts with family and friends. Throw a few steaks on a grill, crack open the cooler, and you have a simple, satisfying meal.

Gas Grill

Horizontal Grill/Smoker

Brazier

Brazier

For some, grilling is an art form; for others, it's the perfect answer to an easy meal. Regardless of your reasons for seeking the sizzle, make sure you choose the grill that's right for you. From high end stainless steel gas grills to a basic hibachi, there's something on the market for everyone.

Gas Grills

Gas grills are the most convenient type of grill. You just turn on the gas, select your temperature, and start cooking. Gas grills can be simple, with a single heating element, or more elaborate, with multiple burners that allow you to regulate heat zones while cooking. Higher-end grills come with helpful features, like side burners and rotisseries.

Charcoal Grills

While gas grills have newer, more high-tech models each year, charcoal grills have changed little since the 1970s. Select a grill with the largest cooking surface that will safely fit in your cooking area.

Charcoal Grills

Charcoal grills come in 3 different styles:

Kettles are larger, with snug-fitting, dome-shape lids. They're the most efficient of the charcoal grills, helping circulate and concentrate the heat so that food cooks more quickly.

Hibachis are small, coverless grills ideal for cooking a couple of skewers or a steak or two. They're usually cast iron and have one to three adjustable grates.

Braziers are the grills of our childhood. Lightweight and portable, they're little more than a charcoal pan with a grate on top. Upgraded versions have adjustable grates for temperature control.

Kettle Grill

Indoor Grilling

Thanks to modern technology you don't have to grill outdoors to get that great grilled taste. If the snow is flying, toss your meat and veggies on an indoor grill or grill pan. Tons of flavor—no frostbite!

Electric Indoor Grill

Indoor Grill Pans

These invaluable stove-top pans are made from a variety of materials, most commonly cast iron and stainless steel. The super heat conducting metals generate quite a bit of warmth, which is why the raised ridges in the pan do such an outstanding job leaving "grill" marks on food. However, because they get so hot, they can also generate a good deal of smoke, so only use in a well-ventilated area.

Grill Pans

Raclette

Electric Indoor Grills

While nothing compares to the aroma, appearance, and flavor (not to mention the experience) of outdoor grilling, you can still get great results when grilling indoors. The perks of using an indoor grilling appliance? They're smokeless, easy to use, easy to clean up (always a plus), quicker to set up, and reasonably priced. While most of the recipes in this book have an alternative "indoor method" that utilizes the oven or stove-top, you can also give any recipe that is grilled directly a try on an indoor grill. Just follow manufacturer's instructions and adjust cooking times accordingly.

Racks

Roasting Rack: Use a roasting rack instead of a traditional rib rack. Flip it over and fill the slots with ribs. Genius!

Raclettes: Cook small pieces of meat, seafood, and vegetables on the top griddle, while preparing traditional raclette cheese below. Serve the two together for an unbeatable flavor combo.

Tools and Toys

Briquettes vs. Lump Coal

Charcoal briquettes can be found year-round, in almost any grocery or hardware store. Before cooking, let the briquettes burn about 25 to 35 minutes until they ash over. This will allow the undesirable chemicals to burn off. Some briquettes come ready to light, with starter fluid built in; others contain wood chips that add subtle flavor to food. Briquettes burn longer than lump coal; however, new briquettes must ash-over before cooking, making them less appealing for foods with longer cook times.

Lump coal or hardwood charcoal, ignites quicker, burns hotter, and is cleaner than briquettes. Once it reaches the desired temperature, you can start cooking without waiting for the coals to ash over. New coals can be added at any time, making it ideal for foods that need to be cooked for an hour or longer. As its popularity grows, lump coal is becoming more widely available.

Long-Handled Tools

Lighter fluid and grilling ingredients

Starting Off

Lighter Fluid: Because it is very FLAMMABLE, read manufacturers' instructions before using. To light, squirt starter fluid on cold charcoal, let it soak in a minute, then ignite the coals with a long match. DO NOT ADD MORE FLUID TO LIT COALS. Let the fluid burn off about 25 minutes before grilling food.

Grilling Essentials: Right before grilling, brush oil or spray nonstick cooking spray on the cold grate of the grill before placing over the coals. Do not spray nonstick cooking spray over hot coals or flame. Use hickory seasoning to obtain authentic grilled taste in any dish.

Long-Handled Tongs, Mitts, Heavy-Duty Aluminum Foil

Cool Tools:

Long-Handled Tongs: A griller's best friend for arranging hot coals, lifting hot grates, or handling food. Avoid using forks—every time meat is poked with a fork, the juices run out!

Long-Handled Spatula: Turn 'em, flip 'em, flop 'em— this utensil will keep your foods on the move, while keeping your hands away from the heat.

Mitts: Too hot to handle! Protect yourself from the flames by covering up.

Instant-Read Thermometer: Absolutely essential for properly cooked meats. Insert thermometer into the thickest part of the meat, away from the bone.

Foil Pans: Inexpensive, disposable, and handy for transporting food. Always use separate pans for raw and cooked food.

Wire Grill Brush: Makes clean-up a breeze.

Fire Extinguisher: Just in case there's a problem!

15

A Grilling Pantry

Flavor! Flavor! Flavor! If it doesn't taste good, it's not worth the effort. Luckily the possibilities are infinite when it comes to store-bought, step-saving ingredients that offer over-the-top taste sensations.

Fruit, preserves, and jellies

Flavorings

Broth and stock

Seasoning blends

Fast Flavor Favorites

Getting big, bold flavors from your grill is easier than ever! Add extra ingredients to store-bought products to create some of the best rubs, marinades, and sauces you've ever tasted.

Rubs are ground spices and herbs mixed together and rubbed onto meat, poultry, and fish. The herb and spice combination depends on the types of meats that they are to be used on. Most contain paprika, chili powder, black pepper, and garlic powder. Wet rubs often start out as dry rubs to which some liquid such as oil, water, beer, or fruit juice has been added as a binder to create a paste.

Marinades are seasoned liquid mixtures used to soak foods to impart flavor. They usually contain an acidic ingredient, such as wine or vinegar, and oil to coat the food. Typically fish and shellfish shouldn't be marinated longer than 30 minutes, while large cuts of beef and pork should be marinated for a minimum of several hours.

Sauce is the finishing touch to any grilled food. Barbecue sauce is the most common sauce used in grilling, but truly there is no end to the saucy combinations you can create. Bottled sauces come in every imaginable color and flavor. When you add your own personal touches (and ingredients), the possibilities are endless.

Chile peppers and chile sauce

Liquor and liqueurs

17

To Know...

Before you start flipping and flaming fabulous food, remember, timing and temperature is everything! Use these charts to help control your grill's heat. And check out my rub and sauce recipes—they're beyond incredible!

Sandra's Sauce & Rub

Sandra's Signature Barbecue Sauce

makes 2¼ cups

YOU WILL NEED
Medium saucepan

1	bottle (12-ounce) chili sauce, *Heinz*®
¼	cup cider vinegar, *Heinz*®
⅓	cup molasses, *Grandma's*®
2	tablespoons Sandra's Sassy All-Purpose Rub (see recipe, right)
2	tablespoons ground black pepper
¼	teaspoon hickory liquid smoke, *Wright's*®

1. In a saucepan over medium heat, stir to combine all ingredients. Simmer for 10 minutes. Remove from heat; cool. Store, covered, in refrigerator for up to 1 week.

Sandra's Sassy All-Purpose Rub

makes about ½ cup

YOU WILL NEED
Medium bowl

2	packets (1.25 ounces each) original chili seasoning, *McCormick*®
3	tablespoons granulated garlic, *Spice Hunter*®
1	tablespoon kosher salt
1	tablespoon salt-free, all-purpose seasoning, *McCormick*®
2	tablespoons sugar

1. In a medium bowl, combine all ingredients. Store in airtight container in cool, dry place or freezer.

The Heat Is On

Gas grills generally come with thermometers, and reliable grill thermometers are available. Modern conveniences aside, the standard is still the "hand method." Hold your hand several inches above the grate and count the number of seconds you can keep it there. Count "one-barbecue, two-barbecue ...," then check the chart below to gauge the temperature.

Heat Level	Temperature	Hand Method
Hot	450° F to 500°F	2 seconds or less
Medium-Hot	400° F to 450°F	3 to 4 seconds
Medium	350° F to 400°F	4 to 5 seconds
Medium-Low	300° F to 350°F	6 to 8 seconds
Low	Below 300° F	More than 10 seconds

Direct Heat Cooking
This is Grilling 101—small pieces of food, such as steaks, are grilled, uncovered, directly over the heat source. For direct cooking, cover the charcoal grate with one layer of briquettes, then pile briquettes into a pyramid in the center of the grate. Apply lighter fluid, let stand for 1 minute, and then light the charcoal. Let the coals burn for 25 to 30 minutes until covered with gray ash. Using long-handled tongs, spread hot coals evenly across the grate (the layer should be 3 inches wider than the food you are cooking). If necessary, oil the cold grate before beginning to cook, then center it over the grill. Never spray the grate with cooking spray when it is over hot coals.

Indirect Heat Cooking
Indirect cooking essentially "bakes" food over a longer period of time. The heat source is off to the side, instead of directly under the food. This method suits larger cuts of meats, as it allows them to cook through before the outside burns.

Indirect cooking on a gas grill: Light the grill, leave one burner off, and place the food on the grate above the unlit burner. Close the grill. Use the temperature control knobs to control the heat.

Indirect cooking on a charcoal grill: Follow "Direct Heat Cooking" directions for arranging and lighting charcoal, using about 50 briquettes. When coals are covered with gray ash, divide them in half and place them on opposite sides of grill. Put a heavy-gauge disposable aluminum pan between the piles to use as a drip pan. Control temperature by opening or closing vents. The more oxygen the coals get, the hotter they'll burn. Add about 10 briquettes to each pile every hour.

Beef and Veal

Few things in life top the delicious perfection of a hot-off-the-grill steak. That smokey beef, cooked to a forget-the-knife tenderness and bursting with flavor, is the quintessential grilling experience to a meat-and-potatoes girl like me. A cut of beef is like a canvas, just waiting for brushstrokes of zesty sauce or fruity marinade to make it a work of culinary art: from rich prime rib rubbed in piquant mustard-ranch seasoning to skirt steak tenderized with teriyaki and beer to thick New York strips treated with a taste of Chocolate Merlot Sauce. Marinades can make tough beef tender and good beef sensational, so really pour it on. Good cooks have always known—the secret's in the sauce!

The Recipes

Chuck Wagon
Brisket

servings 4 **prep time** 15 minutes
grilling time 3½ hours **standing time** 10 minutes

YOU WILL NEED
Foil baking pan
Heavy-duty aluminum foil
Drip pan
1 cup hickory or oak wood chips, soaked in water for
at least 1 hour and drained

1	**6-pound beef brisket**
	Salt and ground black pepper
2	**packets (1.5 ounces each) meat loaf seasoning, *McCormick*®**
1	**bottle (12-ounce) beer**
2	**cups apple cider, *Tree Top*®**
2	**cups BBQ sauce, *KC Masterpiece*®**

INDOOR METHOD:
Preheat oven to
375 degrees F. Prepare
brisket as directed in step
2. Bake in preheated
oven for 2½ to 3 hours.
Remove brisket from
braising liquid and place
on foil-lined baking
sheet. Reduce the
oven temperature to
350 degrees F. Mop
brisket with BBQ sauce
and return to oven. Turn
and mop the brisket two
more times every
15 minutes. Remove
from oven and let stand
10 minutes. Serve
as directed.

1. Set up grill for indirect cooking over medium heat (no heat source under brisket; see page 19).

2. Rinse brisket under cold water and pat dry. Season brisket with salt and pepper and place in foil baking pan. Sprinkle with the meat loaf seasoning and pour beer over top. Add enough apple cider to cover brisket halfway. Cover with heavy-duty aluminum foil.

3. Place on hot grill over drip pan. Cover and grill for 2½ hours. If using charcoal, add 10 briquettes to each pile of coals every hour.

4. Remove brisket and foil pan from grill. Add wood chips to smoke box if using gas grill or place chips onto hot coals if using charcoal. Remove brisket from braising liquid and place directly on grill grate over drip pan. To make the mop sauce, combine 2 cups of braising liquid with BBQ sauce. Mop brisket thoroughly with sauce. Cover grill. Turn and mop brisket every 20 minutes for 1 hour.

5. Transfer the brisket to a cutting board and let stand 10 minutes. Thinly slice against the grain. Serve hot with mop sauce on the side.

Marinated Skirt Steak with Apricots and Tarragon

servings 4 prep time 20 minutes
marinating time 1 hour grilling time 6 minutes
standing time 25 minutes

Skirt steak was generally ignored until fajitas made it famous—a shame because it pulses with flavor when tenderized by a simple fruit marinade. Delicate apricot is an inspired contradiction to pungent garlic and licorice-scented tarragon, creating a tapestry of taste and color as alluring to the eyes as it is to the palate.

YOU WILL NEED
Large zip-top bag
Medium bowl
Oil

1³/₄ **pounds beef skirt steak**
2 **cans (11.5 ounces each) apricot nectar, Kern's®**
2 **packets (1 ounce each) hot taco seasoning, Lawry's®**
2 **teaspoons crushed garlic, Christopher Ranch®**
1 **can (15-ounce) apricot halves, cut up, Del Monte®**
2 **tablespoons slivered almonds, Planters®**
2 **teaspoons chopped fresh tarragon**
1 **teaspoon balsamic vinegar**

1. In a large zip-top bag, combine steak, apricot nectar, taco seasoning, and garlic. Squeeze air out of bag and seal. Gently massage bag to combine ingredients. Marinate in refrigerator for 1 to 3 hours.

2. In a bowl, combine cut-up apricots, slivered almonds, tarragon, and balsamic vinegar; set aside.

3. Set up grill for direct cooking over high heat (see page 19). Oil grate when ready to start cooking. Remove steak from refrigerator; let stand at room temperature about 20 minutes.

4. Remove steak from marinade and discard marinade. Place steak on hot, oiled grill and cook for 3 to 5 minutes per side for medium (160 degrees F). Remove from grill and let stand 5 minutes.

5. To serve, thinly slice steak against the grain. Top with apricot-tarragon mixture; serve hot.

INDOOR METHOD:
Prepare steaks as directed. Preheat broiler. Remove steak from marinade; discard marinade. Place steak on a foil-lined sheet pan or broiler pan. Place steak 6 to 8 inches from heat source and cook for 3 to 5 minutes per side for medium (160 degrees F). Serve as directed.

Teriyaki-Beer
Skirt Steak

servings 6 prep time 20 minutes
marinating time 1 hour grilling time 16 minutes
standing time 5 minutes

YOU WILL NEED
2 large zip-top bags
Oil

1 1/2 pounds beef skirt steak
1/2 cup beer
1/4 cup teriyaki sauce
1/4 cup packed brown sugar
2 tablespoons plus 1 tablespoon black pepper seasoning mix,
Durkee® Grill Creations®
2 red bell peppers, cut into 1/2-inch slices
2 green bell peppers, cut into 1/2-inch slices
2 sweet onions, cut into 1/2-inch slices
3 tablespoons extra-virgin olive oil, *Bertolli®*
2 tablespoons balsamic vinegar
Hawaiian sweet rolls, cut in half

INDOOR METHOD:
Prepare steak and vegetables as directed. In a large skillet, cook vegetables and the vegetable marinade over medium heat for 10 to 15 minutes or until vegetables are just tender. Remove steak from marinade; discard marinade. Place steak on a foil-lined sheet pan or broiler pan. Preheat broiler. Place 6 to 8 inches from heat source and broil for 3 minutes. Turn and broil another 3 to 4 minutes for medium (160 degrees F). Serve as directed.

1. In a zip-top bag, combine steak, beer, teriyaki sauce, brown sugar, and 2 tablespoons seasoning mix. Squeeze air out of bag and seal. Gently massage bag to combine ingredients. Marinate in refrigerator 1 to 3 hours.

2. In another zip-top bag, combine peppers, onions, oil, vinegar, and the remaining 1 tablespoon seasoning mix. Squeeze air out of bag and seal. Gently massage bag to combine ingredients. Marinate in refrigerator 1 to 3 hours.

3. Set up grill for direct cooking over medium-high heat. Oil grate when ready to start cooking.

4. Remove vegetables and steak from marinades; discard marinades. Place vegetables on hot, oiled grill.* Cook for 10 to 15 minutes or until just tender. Remove from grill; set aside. Place steak on hot grill. Cook 3 to 5 minutes per side for medium (160 degrees F). Remove from grill; let stand for 5 minutes. Thinly slice steak at an angle against the grain.

5. To serve, fill Hawaiian sweet rolls with meat and vegetables.

*****NOTE:** If you own a grill wok, use it to cook the vegetables on the grill. If you must put them directly on the grill, be careful not to let the vegetables fall between the grate when grilling.

Kahlúa® Beef Ribs

servings 4 **prep time** 10 minutes
cooking time 10 minutes **grilling time** 2 hours

This sweet Southern recipe is a rib-shack favorite. Slathered with sauce as thick and sultry as a down-home drawl, it cooks until it is fall-off-the-bone tender. Take a bite and the Kahlúa® kicks in, adding just a hint of fine French roast and a shiver of vanilla.

YOU WILL NEED
Small saucepan
Large heavy-duty foil roasting pan
Aluminum foil

1¹/₂ **cups Sandra's Signature Barbecue Sauce (page 19)**
1 **cup *Kahlúa*® (coffee-flavor liqueur)**
1 **rack beef back ribs, cut in 2-bone pieces**

1. Set up grill for indirect cooking over medium heat (no direct heat source under ribs; see page 19).

INDOOR METHOD:
Preheat oven to 375 degrees F. Prepare ribs as directed. Place covered pan in oven for 2 hours. Remove foil and turn ribs meat sides up. Baste with sauce and return to oven for 10 minutes. Turn and baste twice more at 10 minute intervals, ending with meat sides up. Serve as directed.

2. In a saucepan, combine Barbecue Sauce and Kahlúa®. Bring to boil; remove from heat. Reserve ¹/₂ cup of the sauce for basting ribs; set aside.

3. Place ribs, meat sides down, in a large foil roasting pan. Cover with all but reserved ¹/₂ cup sauce. Cover pan with aluminum foil and place on grill away from heat. Cover grill and cook 1¹/₂ to 2 hours. If using charcoal, add 10 briquettes to each pile of coals after an hour.

4. Carefully remove ribs from pan and place, meat sides up, on grill. Baste with reserved ¹/₂ cup sauce; grill 15 minutes. Turn and baste; grill for an additional 15 minutes.

5. Remove ribs from grill. Serve hot.

BBQ Shortribs

servings 4 **prep time** 10 minutes **curing time** 1 hour
standing time 30 minutes **grilling time** 1 1/2 hours

YOU WILL NEED
Small bowl
Heavy-duty aluminum foil
Drip pan

3	**pounds beef shortribs**
1	**packet (1-ounce) onion soup mix, *Lipton*®**
1	**packet (1.31-ounce) sloppy joe mix, *McCormick*®**

1. Rinse shortribs under cold water and pat dry; set aside.

2. In a small bowl, combine onion soup mix and sloppy joe mix. Gently pat dry mix on all sides of ribs until all dry mix is used. Loosely wrap in heavy-duty aluminum foil and cure in refrigerator for 1 to 3 hours.

3. Set up grill for indirect cooking over medium heat (no heat source under ribs; see page 19).

4. Remove ribs from refrigerator; let stand at room temperature about 30 minutes.

5. Place foil-wrapped ribs on hot grill over drip pan. Cover grill and cook for 1 1/2 to 2 hours. If using charcoal, add 10 briquettes to each pile of coals after an hour.

6. Remove from grill and carefully unseal foil. Remove ribs and set aside. Drain juice into a bowl. Allow juice to settle for a few minutes; drain off fat. Discard fat.

7. To serve, plate hot ribs and pour de-fatted juice over top.

INDOOR METHOD:
Place all ingredients plus 1 cup of water in a 5-quart slow cooker. Cover and cook on low-heat setting for 7 to 8 hours or high-heat setting for 3 to 4 hours. Serve as directed.

Prime Rib with Mustard-Ranch Plaster

servings 4 **prep time** 15 minutes
grilling time 1 ½ hours
standing time 10 minutes

YOU WILL NEED
Drip pan
Large bowl
Rubber spatula
Meat thermometer
Strainer

2	**cans (14 ounces each) low-sodium beef broth, *Swanson*®**
1	**large onion, sliced**
1	**4½-pound beef rib roast with bones**
	Salt and ground black pepper
1	**cup spicy brown mustard, *Gulden's*®**
1	**packet (1.6-ounce) ranch dressing, *Hidden Valley*®**
3	**tablespoons cracked black peppercorns**
2	**tablespoons Worcestershire sauce, *Lea & Perrins*®**
1	**tablespoon prepared horseradish, *Morehouse*®**
	Fresh rosemary sprigs (optional)

INDOOR METHOD:
Preheat the oven to 450 degrees F. Place broth and onion in bottom of a roasting pan. Prepare roast as directed and set on wire rack over broth and onion (roast should be 1 to 2 inches above pan). Roast for 30 minutes and then reduce the oven temperature to 325 degrees F. After 1¼ hours begin checking temperature (allow 14 to 16 minutes per pound). Thermometer inserted in the thickest part of the roast (away from bone) should register 135 degrees F for medium-rare and 150 degrees F for medium. Serve as directed.

1. Set up grill for indirect cooking over medium heat (no heat source under meat; see page 19). Add beef broth and sliced onion to drip pan.

2. Rinse roast under cold water and pat dry. Season with salt and pepper. Set aside. In a bowl, combine mustard, ranch dressing mix, cracked peppercorns, Worcestershire sauce, and horseradish. With a rubber spatula, coat roast with mustard plaster.

3. Place roast on hot grill over drip pan. Cover grill and cook for 1 hour. If using a charcoal grill, add 10 briquettes to each pile of coals. Cover grill; continue cooking for 30 minutes to 1 hour or until meat thermometer inserted in the thickest part of the roast (away from bone) registers 135 degrees F for medium-rare or 150 degrees F for medium.

4. Transfer roast to a platter and let stand 10 minutes before carving. Meanwhile, carefully remove drip pan containing beef broth and onion. Pour through a strainer.

5. To serve, garnish roast with onion slices from broth (optional) and fresh rosemary sprigs (optional). Serve broth on the side.

Old No. 7 Tri-Tip

servings 4 **prep time** 10 minutes **marinating time** 1 hour
standing time 25 minutes **grilling time** 24 minutes

Beef's best-kept secret is the tri-tip, a lean cut of meat that England's King Henry VIII fondly dubbed "Sir Loin." To really drink in its rich, regal flavor, give the tri-tip a shot of Jack Daniel's® and apple cider—the liquids moisten as they mellow, bringing out the bold, beefy juices.

YOU WILL NEED
Large zip-top bag
Oil
Meat thermometer
Platter

1	**2^1/$_2$-pound beef tri-tip steak**
2	**tablespoons Sandra's Sassy All-Purpose Rub (page 19)**
1	**cup whiskey, *Jack Daniel's*®**
^{1}/$_2$	**cup apple cider, *Tree Top*®**

INDOOR METHOD:
Prepare steak as directed. Preheat the oven to 450 degrees F. Remove steak from the marinade; discard marinade. Place the steak, fat side up, on a rack in a shallow roasting pan. Roast about 30 minutes for medium or until internal temperature reaches 145 to 150 degrees F. Tent with foil and let stand 10 minutes. Serve as directed.

1. Rinse steak with cold water and pat dry. Pat All-Purpose Rub over steak to cover. Place steak in a large zip-top bag and pour whiskey and cider over top to coat. Squeeze air out of bag and seal. Marinate in refrigerator for 1 to 3 hours.

2. Set up grill for direct cooking over medium-high heat (see page 19). Oil grate when ready to start cooking.

3. Remove steak from refrigerator; let stand at room temperature for 20 to 30 minutes.

4. Remove steak from marinade; discard marinade. Place steak on hot, oiled grill and cook 12 to 15 minutes per side for medium or until internal temperature reaches 145 to 150 degrees F.

5. Transfer steak to a platter and let stand 5 to 10 minutes. Thinly slice steak against the grain and serve hot.

Filet with Roasted Red Pepper Sauce

servings 4 **prep time** 15 minutes
grilling time 12 minutes **standing time** 5 minutes

Filet mignon is the most tender steak you can buy, so let the steak's buttery sublimity be the centerpiece of the meal. Served sizzling in a lively roasted red pepper sauce, topped with refreshing avocado butter, it's dressed to picturesque perfection.

YOU WILL NEED
Oil
Medium bowl
Blender
Small saucepan
Butcher's twine

FOR AVOCADO BUTTER:
1/2 **stick butter, softened**
1/2 **avocado, diced**
1/4 **teaspoon hot pepper sauce,** *Tabasco*®
1/4 **teaspoon salt**
1/4 **teaspoon ground black pepper,** *McCormick*®

FOR ROASTED RED PEPPER SAUCE:
1/2 **cup roasted red bell peppers,** *Mezzetta*®
1/2 **cup Catalina dressing,** *Kraft*®

FOR FILET:
4 **bacon-wrapped beef tenderloin steaks**
1 **packet (0.71-ounce) Montreal steak seasoning,** *McCormick*® *Grill Mates*®

1. Set up grill for direct cooking over high heat (see page 19). Oil grate when ready to start cooking.

2. For Avocado Butter, in a medium bowl, mash the butter and diced avocado with a fork until combined. Stir in hot pepper sauce, salt, and black pepper. Cover and refrigerate until needed.

3. For Roasted Red Pepper Sauce, in a blender, combine roasted red peppers and Catalina dressing. Blend until smooth. Transfer to small saucepan and heat through over low heat.

4. Tie steaks with butcher's twine to maintain shape. Season with steak seasoning. Place on hot, oiled grill; cook for 6 to 8 minutes per side for medium (160 degrees F). Remove from grill; let stand 5 minutes.

5. Carefully remove strings. Top each steak with a spoonful of Avocado Butter. Serve steaks hot in small pools of Roasted Red Pepper Sauce.

INDOOR METHOD:
Prepare steaks as directed. Place steaks on a foil-lined sheet pan or broiler pan. Preheat broiler. Place 6 to 8 inches from heat source. Cook for 8 to 10 minutes per side for medium (160 degrees F). Serve as directed.

Carpetbagger Steaks

servings 4 **prep time** 20 minutes
marinating time 1 hour **grilling time** 10 minutes

This surf and turf classic originated in San Francisco, where a thick steak was sandwiched around seasoned bay oysters. This version takes a Napa Valley twist, featuring mushrooms and bleu cheese instead of oysters.

YOU WILL NEED
Large zip-top bag
Oil
Medium bowl
Toothpicks

FOR STEAKS:
4   beef tenderloin steaks
2   cups red wine
2   tablespoons garlic and herb dressing mix, *Good Seasons*®
2   teaspoons ground black pepper, *McCormick*®

FOR FILLING:
1   jar (4.5-ounce) marinated mushrooms, finely chopped,
      Green Giant®
¹/₄ cup bleu cheese crumbles, *Treasure Cave*®
1   teaspoon Italian salad dressing mix, *Good Seasons*®

Fresh oregano sprigs (optional)

INDOOR METHOD:
Preheat oven to 400 degrees F. Prepare steaks as directed. Remove steaks from marinade; discard marinade. Stuff steaks as directed in step 3. Heat 2 tablespoons oil in oven-proof skillet over medium-high heat. Sear steaks 3 to 4 minutes per side or until browned. Place skillet in oven for 12 to 16 minutes for medium (160 degrees F). Serve as directed.

1. Rinse steaks under cold water and pat dry. Place in zip-top bag and add red wine, dressing mix, and pepper. Squeeze air out of bag and seal. Gently massage bag to combine ingredients. Marinate in refrigerator for 1 to 3 hours.

2. Set up grill for direct cooking over high heat (see page 19). Oil grate when ready to start cooking. In a medium bowl, combine chopped mushrooms, bleu cheese, and Italian seasoning; set aside.

3. Remove steaks from marinade and discard marinade. With a sharp knife, cut a pocket into the side of each steak, being careful not to cut through. Stuff steaks with mushroom mixture and secure with toothpicks. Place on hot, oiled grill and cook 5 to 7 minutes per side for medium (160 degrees F). Remove from grill.

4. To serve, remove toothpicks. Garnish steaks with sprigs of fresh oregano (optional) and serve hot.

New York Strip with Chocolate Merlot Sauce

servings 4 prep time 15 minutes
cooking time 5 minutes grilling time 10 minutes

Semisweet chocolate fuses with fruity Merlot in a fragrant finishing sauce that's a symphony for the senses. Ladled over a prime cut of beef, it's the pièce de résistance for a dress-up dinner. Let it pool on the plate for a presentation that looks—and tastes—deliciously extravagant.

YOU WILL NEED
Oil
Medium saucepan

FOR STEAKS:
4   **1-inch-thick New York beef strip steaks**
     Ground black pepper
1   **packet (1.25-ounce) taco seasoning mix,** *McCormick®*

FOR SAUCE:
2   **tablespoons extra-virgin olive oil,** *Bertolli®*
1   **medium onion, thinly sliced**
2   **teaspoons minced garlic,** *Christopher Ranch®*
1   **jalapeño, finely chopped (see tip, page 202)**
1½ **cups Merlot wine**
3   **ounces semisweet chocolate,** *Nestlé®*
1   **tablespoon onion soup mix,** *Lipton®*

     Fresh basil sprigs (optional)

1. Set up grill for direct cooking over high heat (see page 19). Oil grate when ready to start cooking.

2. Season steaks with black pepper. Rub both sides of steak with entire contents of the taco seasoning packet. Set aside.

3. In a medium saucepan, heat oil over medium-high heat. Add onion, garlic, and jalapeño; cook 5 minutes or until soft. Add Merlot and reduce liquid by half over high heat. Reduce heat to low; stir in chocolate and soup mix. Stir until smooth. Keep warm over low heat.

4. Place steaks on hot, oiled grill. Cook 5 to 7 minutes per side for medium (160 degrees F). Remove from grill.

5. Top each steak with some of the onions from the Chocolate Merlot Sauce and a sprig of fresh basil (optional). Serve sauce on the side.

INDOOR METHOD:
Prepare steaks as directed. Place steaks on a broiler pan. Preheat broiler. Place 6 to 8 inches from heat source and cook 5 minutes. Turn and cook another 4 to 5 minutes for medium (160 degrees F). Serve as directed.

Thai Town New York Strip

servings 4 prep time 10 minutes marinating time 1 hour
standing time 25 minutes grilling time 12 minutes

YOU WILL NEED
Large zip-top bag
Oil

4	**New York beef strip steaks**
³/₄	**cup dry sherry, *Christian Brothers*®**
¹/₄	**cup canola oil, *Wesson*®**
¹/₄	**cup soy sauce, *Kikkoman*®**
2	**tablespoons lime juice, *ReaLime*®**
2	**tablespoons Thai seasoning, *Spice Islands*®**
	Mixed salad greens (optional)

INDOOR METHOD:
Prepare steaks as directed. Preheat broiler. Place steaks on a broiler pan. Place 6 to 8 inches from heat source and broil for 5 minutes. Turn and broil another 4 to 5 minutes for medium (160 degrees F). Serve as directed.

1. Rinse steaks under cold water and pat dry. Put steaks in a zip-top bag and add remaining ingredients, except salad greens. Squeeze air out of bag and seal. Gently massage bag to combine ingredients. Marinate in refrigerator for 1 to 3 hours.

2. Set up grill for direct cooking over high heat (see page 19). Oil grate when ready to start cooking. Remove steaks from refrigerator; let stand at room temperature for 20 to 30 minutes.

3. Remove steaks from marinade; discard marinade. Place steaks on hot, oiled grill and cook for 6 to 8 minutes per side for medium (160 degrees F).

4. Transfer steaks to a platter and let stand 5 minutes before serving. Serve with mixed salad greens (optional).

Gaucho Ribeye Steaks

servings 4 **prep time** 10 minutes **marinating time** 1 hour
standing time 25 minutes **grilling time** 12 minutes

Straight from cattle country, these zesty ribeye steaks are a Southwestern version of *steak au poivre* (pepper steak). Instead of the traditional red wine and peppercorns, they receive their fiery flavor from cocktail sauce and a few chipotle peppers. Serve with mellow sides for a zinger of a meal.

YOU WILL NEED
Large zip-top bag
Oil

4   beef ribeye steaks
1   can (7-ounce) chipotle peppers in adobo sauce, *La Victoria*®
        (see tip, page 202)
1/3   cup cocktail sauce, *Heinz*®
2   tablespoons steak sauce, *Lawry's*®

INDOOR METHOD:
Prepare steaks as directed. Remove steaks from marinade; discard marinade. Place steaks on a broiler pan. Preheat broiler. Place 6 to 8 inches from heat source and cook 5 minutes. Turn and continue cooking 4 minutes for medium (160 degrees F). Serve as directed.

1. Rinse steaks under cold water and pat dry. Place steaks in a zip-top bag and add remaining ingredients. Squeeze air out of bag and seal. Gently massage bag to combine ingredients. Marinate in refrigerator for 1 to 3 hours.

2. Set up grill for direct cooking over high heat (see page 19). Oil grate when ready to start cooking.

3. Remove steaks from refrigerator; let stand at room temperature for 20 to 30 minutes. Remove steaks from marinade; discard marinade. Place steaks on hot, oiled grill and cook for 6 to 8 minutes per side for medium (160 degrees F).

4. Transfer steaks to a platter and let stand 5 minutes before serving.

Smoked Bacon-Wrapped Meat Loaf

servings 4 **prep time** 20 minutes
grilling time 45 minutes **standing time** 10 minutes

Old-fashion meat loaf has become nouveau chic, dished up with a side of nostalgia in some of America's most urbane eateries. Here Grandma's no-nonsense comfort food undergoes a cultural renaissance, wrapped in thick strips of bacon and slow-roasted over wood chips to sear in a distinctive smokehouse flavor.

YOU WILL NEED
Drip pan
1 cup hickory or oak wood chips, soaked in water for at least 1 hour and drained
Large bowl
Foil loaf pan, 8×4×2^1/$_2$ inches
Meat thermometer

1^1/$_2$ **pounds ground beef**
1 **tablespoon Sandra's Sassy All-Purpose Rub (page 19)**
1 **packet (1.1-ounce) beefy onion soup mix, *Lipton*®**
^{1}/$_4$ **cup Sandra's Signature Barbecue Sauce (page 19)**
1 **teaspoon crushed garlic, *Christopher Ranch*®**
^{1}/$_4$ **cup real bacon bits, *Hormel*®**
2 **tablespoons Worcestershire sauce, *Lea & Perrins*®**
1 **egg, lightly beaten**
^{1}/$_2$ **cup bread crumbs, *Progresso*®**
6 **thick-cut bacon slices, *Oscar Mayer*®**
Fresh oregano sprigs (optional)

INDOOR METHOD:
Preheat oven to 400 degrees F. Poke holes in bottom of foil pan. Prepare meat loaf as directed, except add ¼ teaspoon liquid smoke to meat mixture. Shape meat loaf as directed. Place foil pan on a rack in a 13×9-inch baking pan and bake about 45 minutes or until internal temperature reaches 165 degrees F. Serve as directed.

1. Prepare grill for indirect cooking over medium-high heat (no heat source under meat; see page 19). Add wood chips to smoke box if using gas grill or place chips on hot coals if using charcoal. Open grill vents halfway.

2. In a large bowl, combine ground beef and remaining ingredients, except bacon slices and oregano sprigs. Poke several holes into bottom of loaf pan. Lay 4 bacon slices down crosswise in loaf pan, allowing slices to hang over side of pan. Shape meat mixture to fit loaf pan and fold bacon slices to meet over top of meat loaf. Top with remaining 2 bacon slices.

3. Place on hot grill over drip pan; cover grill. Cook for 45 minutes to 1 hour or until internal temperature reaches 165 degrees F. Transfer meat loaf to cutting board and let stand for 10 minutes. Remove from loaf pan and slice. Garnish with fresh oregano sprigs (optional) and serve warm.

Cheesesteak Subs

servings 6 prep time 25 minutes
marinating time 1 hour grilling time 17 minutes

YOU WILL NEED
2 large zip-top bags
2 small bowls
Oil

1$^1/_2$	**pounds beef top round steak**
8	**ounces mushrooms, quartered**
2	**green bell peppers, cut into** $^1/_2$**-inch slices**
1	**large onion, cut into** $^1/_2$**-inch slices**
$^1/_4$	**cup extra-virgin olive oil,** *Bertolli*®
3	**tablespoons Worcestershire sauce,** *Lea & Perrins*®
2	**tablespoons onion soup mix,** *Lipton*®
2	**teaspoons garlic powder,** *McCormick*®
1	**cup mayonnaise,** *Best Foods*® **or** *Hellmann's*®
1	**teaspoon bottled minced garlic,** *Christopher Ranch*®
6	**sandwich rolls, cut in half**
6	**slices provolone cheese,** *Kraft*®

INDOOR METHOD:
Preheat oven to 400 degrees F. Prepare steak and vegetables as directed. Remove meat and vegetables from marinades; discard marinades. Heat a grill pan over high heat; brush lightly with oil. When pan is hot, cook steak 2 to 3 minutes or until cooked through. Transfer steak to a plate; cover with foil. Place vegetables in hot pan. Cook vegetables 5 to 7 minutes or until just tender. Prepare and fill rolls as directed in step 5. Place sandwiches on foil-lined sheet pan and place in oven. Bake about 3 minutes or until cheese has melted. Serve as directed.

1. Slice steak into very thin slices.* Place sliced steak into a zip-top bag; set aside. In another zip-top bag, combine quartered mushrooms, sliced peppers, and sliced onions. Set aside.

2. In a bowl, whisk together olive oil, Worcestershire sauce, onion soup mix, and garlic powder. Pour half of the marinade into each of the zip-top bags. Marinate in refrigerator for 1 to 3 hours.

3. In a bowl, combine mayonnaise and minced garlic. Set aside in refrigerator until needed. Set up grill for direct cooking over medium-high heat (see page 19). Oil grate when ready to start cooking.

4. Remove vegetables and steak from marinades; discard marinades. Place vegetables on hot, oiled grill.** Cook for 10 to 15 minutes or until just tender. Remove from grill and set aside. Grill steak 3 to 4 minutes or until cooked through, turning once. Remove and set aside.

5. Spread sandwich rolls with garlic-mayonnaise mixture. Fill rolls with steak, provolone cheese, and vegetables. Place sandwiches on grill and cover. Cook 2 to 4 minutes or until cheese has melted. Serve warm.

*TIP: Put steak in freezer for 15 minutes for easier slicing.

**NOTE: If you own a grill wok, use it to cook the vegetables on the grill. If you must put them directly on the grill, be careful not to let the vegetables (or beef slices) fall between the grate when grilling.

Peach and Black
Pepper Veal Chops

servings 4   **prep time** 15 minutes
marinating time 3 hours   **cooking time** 10 minutes
standing time 20 minutes   **grilling time** 9 minutes

Something with this much flavor and so simple to make is a find. Strong, coarse peppercorns play off satiny peaches to capture the essence of warmth and light, without overpowering a mellow cut of meat. A fine bourbon glaze finishes it in style.

YOU WILL NEED
   Large zip-top bag
   Small saucepan
   Oil

FOR VEAL CHOPS:
4¹/₂ **pounds veal loin chops**
1   **can (11.5-ounce) peach nectar, *Kern's*®**
1   **packet (1.12-ounce) black peppercorn marinade mix, *Durkee*®**
     ***Grill Creations*®**

FOR GLAZE:
¹/₂   **cup peach jam, *Smucker's*®**
¹/₄   **cup bourbon, *Jim Beam*®**
1   **tablespoon cracked black peppercorns**

INDOOR METHOD:
Prepare and marinate chops as directed. Remove chops from marinade and discard marinade. Pat chops dry with paper towel. Place on foil-lined sheet pan or broiler pan. Place 4 to 6 inches from the heat source and cook 5 to 6 minutes per side or until well seared. Turn and brush with glaze; return to broiler and cook for 1 minute. Turn and brush with glaze; cook for 1 minute more for medium (160 degrees F). To check for doneness, make a small cut in the thickest part of the chop; it should be slightly less done than you like it. Allow the chops to stand for 5 to 10 minutes (internal temperature will continue to rise slightly). Brush chops with more glaze. Serve as directed.

1. In a zip-top bag, combine veal chops, peach nectar, and marinade mix. Squeeze air out of bag and seal. Gently massage bag to coat chops. Marinate in refrigerator 3 to 6 hours.

2. In a small saucepan, combine jam, bourbon, and cracked peppercorns. Bring to a boil over medium heat. Reduce heat and simmer for 10 minutes. Remove from heat; set aside.

3. Set up grill for direct cooking over medium-high heat (see page 19). Oil grate when ready to start cooking.

4. Remove chops from marinade; discard marinade. Let chops stand at room temperature about 20 minutes.

5. Place chops on hot, oiled grill. Cook for 4 to 5 minutes. Turn and brush with glaze. Cook an additional 4 to 5 minutes. Turn and brush with glaze. Cook for 1 minute more for medium (160 degrees F).

6. Remove from heat and brush once more with glaze. Serve hot.

Poultry

Ah, summer Sundays—the pace is slow, the grill is hot, and life is laid back. Chicken is a summer staple on my sister Kimber's grill—a surefire way to give the kids food they love, while letting her husband show off his moves with a spatula. Chicken and turkey are all-around favorites. For fuss-free finger food, dip dark meat wings and legs in buttermilk and bleu cheese or a Tabasco®-Ranch Sauce and cook them fast and hot over a direct flame. Brush white breast meat with a maple-brandy glaze and bake "slow and low" over indirect heat. When the temperature drops outdoors, move the party indoors. Fire up your stovetop grill, and you can savor the flavor of summer Sundays year 'round.

The Recipes

Mesquite-Smoked
Beer Can Chicken

servings 4 **prep time** 15 minutes
curing time 15 minutes
grilling time 1¼ hours
standing time 10 minutes

YOU WILL NEED
Drip pan
1 cup mesquite wood chips, soaked for at least 1 hour and drained
Meat thermometer

1	**4-pound whole roasting chicken**
¼	**cup Sandra's Sassy All-Purpose Rub (page 19)**
1	**can (12-ounce) beer**
	Sandra's Signature BBQ Sauce (page 19)
	(or your favorite BBQ sauce)

1. Set up grill for indirect cooking over medium heat (no heat source under chicken; see page 19).

2. Remove neck and giblets from chicken cavity. Trim excess fat. Rinse inside and outside of chicken with cold water and pat dry.

3. Rub inside and outside of chicken generously with All-Purpose Rub. Let chicken stand for 15 minutes to cure.

4. Open beer; drain one-quarter of the can. Set chicken over the can so that the legs and can form a tripod.

5. Add wood chips to smoke box if using gas grill or place chips on hot coals if using charcoal. Carefully place beer can and chicken on grill over drip pan. Cover grill. Cook 1¼ to 1½ hours or until internal temperature of thigh meat reaches 180 degrees F.

6. Remove chicken from grill and let stand for 10 minutes. Carefully remove beer can and carve chicken.

7. Serve hot with BBQ sauce on side.

INDOOR METHOD:
Preheat oven to 325 degrees F. Prepare the chicken as directed. Place chicken on beer can on a sheet pan. Roast in oven for 1¾ hours or until the internal temperature of thigh meat reaches 180 degrees F. Remove from oven; tent with foil and let stand 10 minutes. Carefully remove beer can and carve chicken. Serve as directed.

Butterflied
Jerk Chicken

servings 4 **prep time** 25 minutes
grilling time 56 minutes
cooking time 8 minutes

YOU WILL NEED
  Kitchen shears
  Small bowl
  Oil
  Small saucepan
  Meat thermometer

FOR CHICKEN:
1   whole roasting chicken
$1/4$ cup Jamaican jerk seasoning, *McCormick*®
$1/2$ teaspoon ground cloves, *McCormick*®
1   teaspoon ground cinnamon, *McCormick*®

FOR GLAZE:
1   cup dark rum, *Myers's*®
$1/4$ cup frozen pineapple juice concentrate, *Old Orchard*®
1   teaspoon Jamaican jerk seasoning, *McCormick*®
1   teaspoon ground cinnamon, *McCormick*®
2   tablespoons packed brown sugar

INDOOR METHOD:
Preheat oven to
425 degrees F. Prepare
chicken as directed. Lay
chicken, skin side up, in
a foil-lined baking pan.
Roast for 30 minutes.
Turn and brush with
glaze. Roast for
10 minutes more. Turn
once more; generously
brush with glaze and
roast an additional 10 to
15 minutes or until
internal temperature of
thigh meat reaches
180 degrees F. Discard
remaining glaze used
as a brush-on. Serve
as directed.

1. To butterfly chicken, remove neck and giblets; cut away excess fat. Using a pair of kitchen shears, cut along both sides of backbone to remove. Turn chicken over, skin side up, and press down between the breasts to break the keel bone (this will allow the chicken to lie flat on grill). Rinse chicken with cold water and pat dry; set aside.

2. In a small bowl, combine jerk seasoning, cloves, and cinnamon. Sprinkle liberally over all sides of chicken; set aside.

3. Set up grill for direct grilling over medium heat (see page 19). Oil grate when ready to start cooking.

4. For glaze, in a small saucepan, combine all glaze ingredients and cook over medium-high heat. Bring to boil; cook for 3 minutes. Remove from heat; divide in half and set aside.

5. Place chicken, skin side up, on hot, oiled grill. Cook for 30 minutes. Turn and cook for 10 minutes. Turn and brush with half of glaze; cook for another 15 minutes or until internal temperature of thigh meat reaches 180 degrees F. Discard remainder of glaze used as brush-on. Turn; brush with remaining half of glaze. Cook for 1 to 2 minutes. Turn and brush with glaze; remove from grill. Carve and serve hot.

Huli Huli
Chicken Halves

servings 4   **prep time** 10 minutes
grilling time 40 minutes

YOU WILL NEED
Oil
Small bowl
Meat thermometer

FOR CHICKEN:
1   whole roasting chicken, cut in half
¹/₄   cup Asian seasoning blend, *Emeril's® Asian Essence*

FOR HULI HULI SAUCE:
¹/₂   cup Hawaiian marinade, *Lawry's®*
¹/₂   cup soy sauce, *Kikkoman®*
¹/₂   cup low-sodium chicken broth, *Swanson®*
¹/₂   cup dry sherry, *Christian Brothers®* (or apple cider)
Grilled fresh pineapple slices (optional)

INDOOR METHOD:
Preheat oven to 325 degrees F. Prepare the chicken as directed. Lay chicken, skin side up, on a foil-lined sheet pan. Roast for 1½ hours or until internal temperature of thigh meat reaches 180 degrees F, basting with Huli Huli Sauce every 15 minutes until nearly done. Discard any remaining sauce. Serve as directed.

1. Set up grill for direct grilling over medium heat (see page 19). Oil grate when ready to start cooking.

2. Rinse chicken halves with cold water and pat dry. Sprinkle Asian seasoning blend liberally over both sides of chicken halves; set aside.

3. In a small bowl, mix together Hawaiian marinade, soy sauce, broth, and sherry.

4. Place chicken on hot, oiled grill. Cook chicken for 20 to 25 minutes per side, turning every 10 minutes. Liberally baste chicken with Huli Huli Sauce after each turn. Discard any remaining sauce. Cook chicken until internal temperature of thigh meat reaches 180 degrees F.

5. Serve hot with grilled fresh pineapple slices (optional).

Southwestern Chicken with Mango-Peach Salsa

servings 4 **prep time** 15 minutes
grilling time 10 minutes

YOU WILL NEED
Oil
Small bowl
Medium bowl

FOR CHICKEN:
4   skinless, boneless chicken breast halves
3   tablespoons Sandra's Sassy All-Purpose Rub (page 19)
1   tablespoon ground cumin, *McCormick*®
¹/₂   teaspoon cayenne, *McCormick*®

FOR MANGO-PEACH SALSA:
8   ounces frozen peach slices, diced, *Dole*®*
8   ounces frozen mango chunks, diced, *Dole*®*
1   jalapeño, finely chopped (see tip, page 202)
¹/₄   cup chopped fresh cilantro
2   tablespoons lime juice, *ReaLime*®
¹/₄   teaspoon salt

1. Set up grill for direct grilling over medium heat (see page 19). Oil grate when ready to start cooking.

2. Rinse chicken breast halves with cold water and pat dry; set aside.

3. In a small bowl, mix together All-Purpose Rub, cumin, and cayenne. Gently pat onto all sides of chicken breasts, using all the rub mix; set aside while preparing salsa.

4. For Mango-Peach Salsa, in a medium bowl, toss to combine peaches, mango, jalapeño, cilantro, lime juice, and salt. Cover; set aside.

5. Place chicken on hot, oiled grill. Cook for 5 to 6 minutes per side or until chicken is no longer pink and juices run clear (170 degrees F). Serve with salsa.

*TIP: It is easier to dice frozen fruit while it is still frozen.

INDOOR METHOD:
Preheat oven to 350 degrees F. Prepare the chicken breasts as directed. Place chicken breasts on a foil-lined sheet pan and roast for 35 to 40 minutes or until chicken is no longer pink and juices run clear (170 degrees F). Serve as directed.

Margarita
Chicken Breasts

servings 4 **prep time** 10 minutes
marinating time 1 hour
standing time 30 minutes
grilling time 36 minutes

YOU WILL NEED
Small bowl
Large zip-top bag
Oil

4	**bone-in chicken breast halves**
1	**can (10-ounce) frozen margarita mix, thawed,** *Bacardi®*
²/₃	**cup tequila**
¹/₂	**cup chopped fresh cilantro**
2	**tablespoons chicken seasoning,** *McCormick® Grill Mates®*

1. Rinse chicken breasts with cold water and pat dry; set aside.

2. For marinade, in a small bowl, combine margarita mix, tequila, cilantro, and chicken seasoning. Place chicken in large zip-top bag; pour marinade over chicken. Squeeze air out of bag and seal. Gently massage bag to coat chicken. Marinate in refrigerator for 1 to 2 hours.

3. Set up grill for direct cooking over medium heat (see page 19). Oil grate when ready to start cooking. Remove chicken from refrigerator; let stand at room temperature about 30 minutes. Remove chicken from marinade; discard marinade.

4. Place chicken on hot, oiled grill and cook 18 to 22 minutes per side or until chicken is no longer pink and juices run clear (170 degrees F). Remove from grill; serve hot.

INDOOR METHOD:
Prepare chicken breasts as directed. Preheat oven to 375 degrees F. Remove chicken breasts from marinade; discard marinade. Place chicken breasts on foil-lined sheet pan. Roast for 45 to 50 minutes or until chicken is no longer pink and juices run clear (170 degrees F). Serve as directed.

Provence-Style Chicken Breasts

servings 4 prep time 15 minutes
marinating time 1 hour
standing time 30 minutes
grilling time 10 minutes

YOU WILL NEED
Waxed paper
Small bowl
Large zip-top bag
Oil

4	**boneless, skinless chicken breast halves**
1/2	**cup light olive oil, *Bertolli*®**
2	**tablespoons herbes de Provence, *Spice Island*®**
2	**tablespoons lemonade concentrate, *Minute Maid*®**
1	**tablespoon citrus herb seasoning, *Spice Island*®**
1	**tablespoon champagne vinegar, *O Olive Oil*®**

INDOOR METHOD:
Prepare chicken as directed. Preheat broiler. Remove chicken breast halves from marinade; discard marinade. Place chicken breast halves on foil-lined sheet pan or broiler pan. Place 6 to 8 inches from heat source. Cook for 2 to 4 minutes per side or until meat is no longer pink and juices run clear (170 degrees F). Serve as directed.

1. Rinse chicken breasts with cold water and pat dry. Place chicken between sheets of waxed paper and pound to 1/2 inch thickness.

2. In a small bowl, stir together remaining ingredients. Pour marinade mixture into zip-top bag and add chicken. Squeeze out air and seal bag. Marinate in refrigerator 1 to 2 hours.

3. Set up grill for direct grilling over medium heat (see page 19). Oil grate when ready to start cooking. Remove chicken from refrigerator; let stand at room temperature about 30 minutes. Remove chicken from marinade; discard marinade.

4. Place chicken on hot, oiled grill and cook 5 to 6 minutes per side or until chicken is no longer pink and juices run clear (170 degrees F). Remove from grill; serve hot.

Lemon-Herb Butter-Basted Chicken

servings 4 **prep time** 10 minutes
grilling time 36 minutes

YOU WILL NEED
Oil
Small saucepan

1	**stick butter (1/2 cup)**
1 1/2	**tablespoons lemon-herb chicken sauce mix, *McCormick*®**
2	**tablespoons lemon juice, *ReaLemon*®**
1	**3 1/2-pound whole chicken, cut up**
	Garlic salt, *Lawry's*®
	Lemon pepper, *Lawry's*®
	Fresh herbs (such as sage, thyme, and tarragon) (optional)
	Lemon slices (optional)

INDOOR METHOD:
Preheat broiler. Prepare chicken as directed. Place chicken on foil-lined sheet pan or broiler pan. Place 6 to 8 inches from heat source. Cook about 15 to 20 minutes per side or until chicken is no longer pink and juices run clear (170 degrees F), basting with butter mixture every few minutes until last 2 minutes of cooking. Discard remaining butter mixture. Serve as directed.

1. Set up grill for direct cooking over medium heat (see page 19). Oil grate when ready to start cooking.

2. In a small saucepan, melt butter over medium heat. Stir in sauce mix and lemon juice. Cook 1 minute. Remove from heat; set aside.

3. Rinse chicken pieces with cold water and pat dry. Season with garlic salt and lemon pepper.

4. Place chicken on hot, oiled grill. Cook for 18 to 22 minutes per side or until chicken is no longer pink and juices run clear (180 degrees F), basting with butter mixture every few minutes until last 2 minutes of cooking. Discard remaining butter mixture. Remove from grill

5. Garnish chicken with herbs and lemon slices (optional). Serve hot.

Tandoori Chicken Thighs

servings 4 prep time 10 minutes
marinating time 2 hours
standing time 30 minutes
grilling time 36 minutes

YOU WILL NEED
Large bowl
Plastic wrap
Oil
Meat thermometer

8	**chicken thighs**
1½	**cups plain yogurt, *Dannon*®**
2	**teaspoons garam masala*, *Spice Hunter*®**
2	**teaspoons paprika**
1	**teaspoon minced ginger, *Christopher Ranch*®**
1	**teaspoon crushed garlic, *Christopher Ranch*®**

INDOOR METHOD:
Prepare chicken as directed. Preheat oven to 425 degrees F. Place chicken on foil-lined sheet pan. Roast for 30 minutes or until internal temperature reaches 180 degrees F. Serve as directed.

1. Rinse chicken thighs with cold water and pat dry.

2. In a large bowl, combine yogurt, garam masala, paprika, ginger, and garlic; stir until smooth. Add chicken; toss to coat. Cover with plastic wrap and marinate in the refrigerator at least 2 hours, preferably overnight.

3. Set up grill for direct cooking over medium heat (see page 19). Oil grate when ready to start cooking. Remove chicken from refrigerator; let stand at room temperature about 30 minutes.

4. Place chicken on hot, oiled grill. Cook for 18 to 22 minutes per side or until internal temperature reaches 180 degrees F. Serve hot.

*NOTE: Garam masala is a blend of aromatic spices used in Indian cooking. It can be found in the spice section of the grocery store.

Blazin' Buttermilk Wings

servings 4 prep time 10 minutes
marinating time 3 hours
standing time 30 minutes
grilling time 12 minutes

Wing worshippers still flock to the Anchor Bar in Buffalo, New York, where spicy wings were first sauced up and served. Marinated in tangy buttermilk and "hotted up" with Tabasco®, this variation of the original is party-food heaven. Surround them with celery sticks, cucumber slices, and a side of chilled bleu cheese dressing for dipping.

YOU WILL NEED
Large bowl
Plastic wrap
Oil

1	**quart buttermilk**
2	**packets (1.06 ounces each) buffalo wing seasoning, *McCormick*®**
¹⁄₄	**cup hot pepper sauce, *Tabasco*®**
4	**pounds chicken wings**
	Bleu cheese dressing, for dipping, *Bob's Big Boy*®
	Celery sticks
	Cucumber slices

1. In a large bowl, combine buttermilk, wing seasoning, and hot pepper sauce. Add wings; toss to coat. Cover with plastic wrap and marinate in the refrigerator at least 3 hours, preferably overnight.

2. Set up grill for direct cooking over medium-high heat (see page 19). Oil grate when ready to start cooking.

3. Remove wings from refrigerator; let stand at room temperature about 30 minutes. Remove from marinade; discard marinade.

4. Place on hot, oiled grill. Cook for 12 to 18 minutes or until cooked through, turning occasionally.

5. Serve with bleu cheese dressing, celery sticks, and cucumber slices.

INDOOR METHOD:
Prepare wings as directed. Preheat broiler. Place wings on foil-lined sheet pan or broiling pan. Place 6 to 8 inches from heat source. Cook for 15 to 20 minutes or until cooked through, turning occasionally. Serve as directed.

Hot Legs with Tabasco®-Ranch Sauce

servings 8 **prep time** 10 minutes
marinating time 2 hours
standing time 20 minutes
grilling time 10 minutes

Drumettes are America's favorite "appeteasers," a saucy, finger-lickin' snack served scorching hot. Given a zip of red wine vinegar and Tabasco® sauce and dipped in creamy ranch dressing, they're a ringer for the ones at sports bars. Serve these small wonders in big portions—they'll go fast!

YOU WILL NEED
Large bowl
Small bowl
Oil

1   packet hot taco seasoning, *McCormick®*
3   tablespoons canola oil, *Wesson®*
2   tablespoons red wine vinegar, *Pompeii®*
2   teaspoons *Tabasco®* (hot pepper sauce)
4   pounds chicken wing drumettes
1   cup ranch salad dressing, *Hidden Valley®*
1   teaspoon *Tabasco®* (hot pepper sauce)
     Celery sticks

INDOOR METHOD:
Prepare drumettes as directed. Remove from marinade and pat dry. Discard marinade. Heat 1 to 2 inches of vegetable oil to 375 degrees F over high heat in a deep skillet or Dutch oven. Add a single layer of chicken drumettes. Cook 12 to 14 minutes or until golden and crisp, turning occasionally. Remove from skillet and drain on paper towels. Repeat with remaining drumettes. Serve as directed.

1. In a large bowl, combine taco seasoning, canola oil, red wine vinegar, and the 2 teaspoons Tabasco®. Add drumettes; toss to combine. Cover and marinate in refrigerator for 2 to 4 hours.

2. For the Tabasco®-Ranch Sauce, in a small bowl, stir to combine ranch dressing and the 1 teaspoon Tabasco®. Cover and refrigerate until ready to serve.

3. Set up grill for direct cooking over medium-high heat (see page 19). Oil grate when ready to start cooking. Remove chicken from refrigerator; let stand at room temperature for 20 to 30 minutes. Remove chicken from marinade; discard marinade.

4. Place drumettes on hot, oiled grill. Cook 10 to 15 minutes or until cooked through, turning often to cook evenly. Remove from grill.

5. Serve hot with Tabasco®-Ranch Sauce and celery sticks.

Cinnamon-Spiced Turkey Breast with Cranberry-Orange Sauce

servings 4 prep time 20 minutes
grilling time 1 hour
standing time 10 minutes

The experience starts on the grill with the perfume of warm baking spices blending with the fruity aroma of citrus and the tantalizing tang of BBQ, topped off with the succulent scent of roasting turkey. On the tongue, it's an explosion of flavors—sweet, salty, spicy, and tangy—interplaying into a harmonious whole.

YOU WILL NEED
Small bowl
Small saucepan
Oil
Meat thermometer

FOR TURKEY:
3 tablespoons Sandra's Sassy All-Purpose Rub (page 19)
1 tablespoon cinnamon, *McCormick*®
1 tablespoon packed brown sugar
2 pound whole boneless turkey breast half (fillet)

FOR CRANBERRY-ORANGE SAUCE:
3/4 cup BBQ sauce, *KC Masterpiece*®
1/2 cup jellied cranberry sauce, *Ocean Spray*®
2 tablespoons frozen orange juice concentrate, thawed, *Minute Maid*®

INDOOR METHOD:
Preheat oven to 350 degrees F. Prepare turkey as directed. Place on foil-lined sheet pan. Roast for 50 to 60 minutes or until internal temperature reaches 170 degrees F, brushing with Cranberry-Orange Sauce every 15 minutes. Remove from oven. Let stand 10 minutes. Bring the remaining sauce to boiling; cook for 1 minute. Slice turkey and serve as directed.

1. In a small bowl, mix together All-Purpose Rub, cinnamon, and brown sugar; set aside. Rinse turkey breast half with cold water and pat dry. Gently pat rub mixture all over turkey, using all of the rub mix. Let turkey cure while preparing sauce.

2. For Cranberry-Orange Sauce, in a small saucepan, combine sauce ingredients. Cook over medium heat, stirring until smooth. Bring to simmer and remove from heat.

3. Set up grill for direct cooking over medium heat (see page 19). Oil grate when ready to start cooking. Place turkey breast half on hot, oiled grill. Cook about 1 hour or until internal temperature reaches 170 degrees F, turning occasionally. Baste turkey with Cranberry-Orange Sauce after each turn up to the last 5 minutes of cooking.

4. Remove from grill and let stand 10 minutes. Meanwhile, bring remaining Cranberry-Orange Sauce to boiling; cook for 1 minute. Slice turkey into 1/4-inch-thick pieces. Serve hot with sauce on the side.

Herb-Crusted Turkey Breast with Maple-Brandy Glaze

servings 4   **prep time** 15 minutes
grilling time 1 hour   **standing time** 10 minutes

This gorgeously grilled turkey breast is the picture of reserved elegance, but the reserve hardly applies to taste. It's saturated with an opulence of flavors. Ribbons of maple syrup and apple juice are woven into a brandy glaze that is sweet contrast to a crust of French herbs and Dijon mustard.

YOU WILL NEED
Small saucepan
Small bowl
Drip pan
Meat thermometer

FOR MAPLE-BRANDY GLAZE:
$1/2$ cup brandy, *E & J*®
$1/3$ cup real maple syrup, *Springfield*®
1   tablespoon frozen apple juice concentrate, *Langer's*®
2   teaspoons Dijon mustard, *Grey Poupon*®

FOR HERB-CRUSTED TURKEY BREAST:
2   tablespoons herbes de Provence, *Spice Island*®
1   tablespoon Dijon mustard, *Grey Poupon*®
1   tablespoon extra-virgin olive oil, *Bertolli*®
1   2-pound boneless turkey breast half (fillet)
    Salt and ground black pepper

INDOOR METHOD:
Preheat oven to 350 degrees F. Prepare turkey breast as directed. Place on foil-lined sheet pan. Roast for 50 to 60 minutes or until internal temperature is 170 degrees F. During the last 15 minutes of roasting, brush with Maple-Brandy Glaze every 5 minutes. Let stand 10 minutes before slicing. Serve as directed.

1. Set up grill for indirect cooking over medium heat (no heat source under turkey breast; see page 19).

2. For Maple-Brandy Glaze, in a small saucepan, reduce brandy by half (about $1/4$ cup) over medium-high heat. Add remaining glaze ingredients and bring to a boil. Remove from heat; set aside.

3. For Herb-Crusted Turkey Breast, in a small bowl, stir to combine herbes de Provence, mustard, and olive oil; set aside. Rinse turkey breast with cold water and pat dry. Season with salt and pepper. Brush herb mixture over turkey breast, coating thoroughly.

4. Place turkey breast on hot grill over a drip pan. Cook about 1 hour or until internal temperature reaches 170 degrees F. During the last 15 minutes of grilling, brush turkey with glaze every 5 minutes.

5. Remove from grill and let stand 10 minutes before slicing. Serve hot.

Smoked Game Hens with Tangerine Glaze

servings 4 **prep time** 10 minutes
grilling time 1 hour
standing time 10 minutes

YOU WILL NEED

Drip pan
1 cup hickory chips, soaked in water for at least 1 hour and drained
Small saucepan
Meat thermometer

3	**Cornish game hens, *Tyson*®**
	Salt and ground black pepper
1¹/₂	**cups tangerine juice, *Odwalla*®**
2	**tablespoons honey, *Sue Bee*®**
2	**tablespoons ginger teriyaki marinade mix, *McCormick*® *Grill Mates*®**

1. Set up grill for indirect cooking (no heat source under games hens; see page 19).

2. Cut hens in half with kitchen shears, removing backbone. Rinse hens with cold water and pat dry. Season both sides of halves with salt and pepper.

3. Add some of the wood chips to smoke box if using gas grill or place chips on hot coals if using charcoal. Place hen halves, bone sides down, on hot grill over drip pan. Cover grill. Cook 1 hour to 1¹/₄ hours or until internal temperature of thigh meat reaches 180 degrees F.

4. Meanwhile in a small saucepan, reduce tangerine juice by half (about ³/₄ cup) over medium-high heat. Stir in honey and teriyaki mix. Bring to boil; remove from heat.

5. During the last 15 minutes of cooking, brush hens liberally with glaze every 5 minutes.

6. Remove from grill and let stand 10 minutes before serving; brush with glaze once more. Serve hot.

INDOOR METHOD:
Preheat oven to 425 degrees F. Prepare hens as directed. Place hens in a roasting pan, skin sides up. Pour glaze over hens. Roast for 40 to 45 minutes or until internal temperature of thigh meat reaches 180 degrees F, rebrushing with glaze from the pan several times during the last 10 minutes of roasting. Let stand 10 minutes. Serve as directed.

Five Spice-Rubbed Duck Breast with Cherry Salsa

servings 4 **prep time** 15 minutes
curing time 15 minutes
grilling time 16 minutes
standing time 5 minutes

Dark, smokey, and fruity, this duck is divine. The cool mint and cherry of the salsa are balanced by a bold blend of aromatic Asian spices released with the heat.

YOU WILL NEED
Oil
Medium bowl
Meat thermometer

FOR CHERRY SALSA:
1   pound frozen pitted cherries, chopped*
¹/₄ cup mint leaves, finely chopped
1   jalapeño, seeded and finely chopped (see tip, page 202)
2   tablespoons balsamic vinaigrette, *Newman's Own*®

FOR DUCK BREASTS:
2   muscovy duck breasts
     Salt and ground black pepper
2   tablespoons five-spice powder, *McCormick*®

INDOOR METHOD:
Prepare duck breasts as directed. Place the duck breasts, skin sides down, in an un-oiled skillet. Cook over medium-low heat for 10 to 12 minutes as fat renders from duck breast. Increase heat to medium and turn breasts. Continue cooking 10 to 12 minutes more for medium. Let stand 5 minutes before slicing. Serve as directed.

1. Set up grill for direct cooking over medium heat (see page 19). Oil grate when ready to start cooking.

2. For Cherry Salsa, in a medium bowl, toss to combine chopped cherries, mint, jalapeño, and vinaigrette; set aside.

3. Rinse duck breasts with cold water and pat dry. Score (make slices in) skin several times with a knife. Season with salt and pepper; rub completely with five-spice powder. Let cure 15 minutes.

4. Place duck breasts, skin sides down, on hot, oiled grill. Cook for 10 minutes, watching for flare-ups. Turn and cook an additional 6 to 8 minutes or until internal temperature reaches 155 degrees F.

5. Remove from grill and let stand 5 minutes before slicing. Serve hot with Cherry Salsa.

*TIP: Cherries are easier to chop when still frozen.

Pork and Lamb

Chicken has long been one of a chef's best buddies, but the other white meat deserves its turn on the grill. Pork and lamb are often thought of as "restaurant foods," difficult dishes best left to professional chefs. I used to shy away from them, too, until I figured out a foolproof way to grill them at home. Inventive combinations mix the subtle with the bold—tangerine and teriyaki on babyback ribs or molasses and Jack Daniel's® whiskey on a rack of lamb. Every dish is simple, but special, from good old Southern traditions, like Memphis-style BBQ, to trendsetting sophisticates, such as mai tai skewers. Whether you're looking for something uptown or down-home, playing with fire definitely has its rewards.

The Recipes

Sweet and Smokey Spareribs

servings 4 **prep time** 10 minutes
grilling time 2½ hours **cooking time** 20 minutes

Southern hospitality demands that everybody have a drink—even the ribs. Here, tradition calls for a cup of Kahlúa®. The chemistry is intoxicating—deep, dark coffee-flavor liqueur blending voluptuously with sweet, sassy BBQ sauce. Hickory-smoked over wood chips, it's a finger-lickin' favorite.

YOU WILL NEED
Drip pan
2 cups hickory chips, soaked in water for at least 1 hour and drained
Rib rack (optional)
Medium saucepan

FOR RIBS:
2   racks pork spareribs
1   cup Sweet & Sassy All-Purpose Rub (page 19)

FOR SAUCE:
1   bottle (12-ounce) chili sauce, *Heinz*®
⅓   cup coffee-flavor liqueur, *Kahlúa*®
¼   cup cider vinegar, *Heinz*®
2   tablespoons Sandra's Sassy All-Purpose Rub (page 19)
2   tablespoons ground black pepper, *McCormick*®
¼   teaspoon hickory liquid smoke, *Wright's*®

1. With a knife, remove membrane from backs of ribs. Rinse ribs under cold water; pat dry. Rub the 1 cup of the All-Purpose Rub onto both sides of ribs. Set aside.

INDOOR METHOD:
Preheat oven to 350 degrees F. Cut racks of ribs into serving portions and prepare with rub as directed. Place ribs in a large shallow roasting pan and bake for 1 hour. Prepare sauce as directed. Continue baking ribs for 1 hour longer, brushing with sauce every 10 to 15 minutes. Serve hot with remaining sauce on the side.

2. Set up grill for indirect cooking over medium heat (no heat source under ribs; see page 19). Add some of the wood chips to smoke box if using gas grill or place chips on hot coals if using charcoal.

3. Place ribs in rib rack on hot grill over drip pan (or place ribs, bone sides down, directly on hot grill). Cover grill and cook about 2½ to 3 hours or until ribs are tender. If using charcoal, add 10 briquettes and a handful of soaked wood chips to coals every hour. For a gas grill, add some wood chips to the smoke box every hour.

4. In a saucepan, combine sauce ingredients over medium heat. Bring to a boil. Reduce heat and simmer for 15 minutes; set aside. About 30 minutes before ribs are done, remove ribs from rib rack and place, meat sides down, on grill. Generously brush with sauce; stack ribs over drip pan. Cover and grill 10 minutes. Turn ribs every 10 minutes, brushing with sauce and restacking. Transfer cooked ribs to platter and cut into portion sizes. Serve with remaining sauce.

Tangerine Teriyaki Ribs

servings 4 **prep time** 15 minutes
marinating time 1 hour **standing time** 30 minutes
cooking time 20 minutes **grilling time** 2 hours

YOU WILL NEED
Drip pan
Large shallow pan
Small bowl
Rib rack (optional)
2 cups hickory chips, soaked in water for at least 1 hour and drained
Medium saucepan

3   **racks pork babyback ribs**
3   **cups tangerine juice,** *Harvest*®
2   **packets (1.06 ounces each) ginger teriyaki marinade mix,**
       McCormick® *Grill Mates*®
1   **cup BBQ sauce,** *KC Masterpiece*®

1. With a knife, remove membrane from the backs of ribs. Rinse racks and pat dry. Place ribs in a large shallow pan. In a small bowl, combine 2 cups of the tangerine juice and both packets of ginger teriyaki mix. Pour marinade mixture over ribs. Cover and marinate in the refrigerator for 1 to 3 hours.

2. Set up grill for indirect cooking over medium heat (no heat source under ribs; see page 19). Remove ribs from refrigerator; let stand at room temperature about 30 minutes.

3. Add some of the soaked wood chips to the smoke box if using a gas grill or place chips on hot coals if using charcoal. Remove ribs from marinade mixture; do not discard marinade. Place ribs in rib rack on hot grill over drip pan (or place ribs, bone sides down, directly on hot grill). Cover grill. Cook 2 to 2½ hours. Rotate ribs around rack every 30 minutes. If using charcoal, add 10 briquettes and a handful of soaked wood chips to each pile of coals every hour. If using a gas grill, add a handful of soaked wood chips to the smoke box every hour.

4. Meanwhile, for the sauce, pour the rib marinade into a medium saucepan. Bring to a boil over high heat; cook for 5 minutes. Reduce heat to medium and add the remaining 1 cup tangerine juice and BBQ sauce. Simmer 10 minutes; remove from heat.

5. About 20 minutes before ribs are done, remove ribs from rib rack and place, meat sides down, on grill. Generously brush with sauce; stack ribs over drip pan. Cover and cook 10 minutes. Turn ribs; brush with additional sauce and restack. Cook an additional 10 minutes. Cut into portion sizes. Serve hot with sauce on the side.

INDOOR METHOD:
Prepare ribs as directed. Preheat oven to 350 degrees F. Remove ribs from marinade; reserve marinade. Place ribs, meat sides up, in a shallow roasting pan. Cover tightly with foil. Bake for 1 hour. Meanwhile, make sauce as directed in step 4. Remove ribs from oven and carefully drain fat from roasting pan. Continue baking ribs, uncovered, for 30 to 45 minutes more or until tender, turning and brushing occasionally with sauce during the last 20 minutes of cooking. Serve as directed.

Cherry Coke®
Babyback Ribs

servings 4 **prep time** 15 servings
grilling time 2 hours
cooking time 15 minutes

YOU WILL NEED

Drip pan
Small bowl
Rib rack (optional)
2 cups hickory chips soaked in water at least 1 hour and drained
Medium saucepan

FOR RIBS:
3   racks pork babyback ribs
1/3   cup Sandra's Sassy All-Purpose Rub (page 19)
2   tablespoons teriyaki mix, *Kikkoman*®

FOR SAUCE:
1   cup *Cherry Coke*® (cherry-flavor cola)
1   cup BBQ sauce, *KC Masterpiece*®
1/3   cup cherry preserves, *Tropical*®
2   tablespoons teriyaki mix, *Kikkoman*®

1. Set up grill for indirect cooking over medium heat (no heat source under ribs; see page 19). With a knife, remove membrane from the backs of ribs. Rinse racks and pat dry.

2. In a small bowl, combine All-Purpose Rub with 2 tablespoons teriyaki mix. Pat seasoning onto both sides of the ribs.

3. Add some of the soaked wood chips to the smoke box if using a gas grill or place chips on each pile of hot coals if using charcoal. Place ribs in rib rack on hot grill over drip pan (or place ribs, bone sides down, directly on hot grill). Cover grill. Cook 2 to 2½ hours. Rotate ribs around rack every 30 minutes. If using charcoal, add 10 briquettes and some soaked wood chips to each pile of coals every hour. If using a gas grill, add a handful of soaked wood chips to the smoke box every hour.

4. Meanwhile, in a medium saucepan, combine sauce ingredients. Bring to a boil over medium heat. Reduce heat and simmer 10 minutes; remove from heat.

5. About 20 minutes before ribs are done, remove ribs from rib rack and place, meat sides down, on grill. Generously brush with sauce and stack ribs over drip pan. Cover and cook 10 minutes. Turn ribs; brush with additional sauce and re-stack. Cook 10 minutes. Remove from grill and cut into portion sizes. Serve hot with remaining sauce on the side.

INDOOR METHOD:
Prepare ribs as directed. Preheat oven to 350 degrees F. Place ribs, meat sides up, on a rack in a shallow roasting pan. Tightly cover with foil. Bake for 1 hour. Meanwhile, make sauce as directed in step 4. Remove ribs from oven and carefully drain fat from roasting pan. Continue baking ribs, uncovered, for 30 to 45 minutes more or until tender, turning and brushing occasionally with sauce during the last 20 minutes of baking. Serve as directed.

Memphis-Style BBQ Pork Shoulder

servings 6 **prep time** 15 minutes
curing time 1 hour **standing time** 30 minutes
cooking time 15 minutes **grilling time** 4 hours

YOU WILL NEED
Small bowl
Large zip-top bag
Spray bottle
Medium saucepan
Hickory wood chips, soaked in water for at least 1 hour and drained
Large bowl

FOR PORK:
3$^{1}/_{2}$ pounds pork shoulder roast
$^{1}/_{4}$ cup Sandra's Sassy All-Purpose Rub (page 19)
1 tablespoon dry mustard, *McCormick*®
12 slices Texas toast or thick white bread, toasted

FOR SPRAY MOP:
1 cup apple cider, *Tree Top*®
$^{1}/_{2}$ cup whiskey, *Jack Daniel's*®

FOR SAUCE:
2 cups BBQ sauce, *KC Masterpiece*®
1 cup cola, *Pepsi*®
$^{1}/_{2}$ cup yellow mustard, *French's*®
$^{1}/_{2}$ cup steak sauce, *Lawry's*®

1. Rinse pork roast and pat dry. In a bowl, combine All-Purpose Rub and dry mustard. Pat roast with rub mixture, using all of the rub. Place in zip-top bag. Squeeze out air and seal. Let cure in refrigerator for 1 to 3 hours. Remove from refrigerator; let stand at room temperature about 30 minutes.

2. Set up grill for indirect cooking over medium heat (no heat source under roast; see page 19). In a spray bottle, combine apple cider and whiskey; set aside. In a medium saucepan, combine sauce ingredients. Bring to a boil; reduce heat and simmer for 10 minutes. Remove from heat; set aside until needed.

3. Add some of the soaked wood chips to the smoke box if using a gas grill or place chips on hot coals if using charcoal. Place roast on hot grill over drip pan. Cover grill. Cook 4 to 6 hours or until roast is very tender. Spray roast with apple-whiskey mixture every hour and every 15 minutes the last hour of cooking. If using charcoal, add 10 briquettes to each pile of coals every hour, along with a handful of wood chips. If using a gas grill, add a handful of soaked wood chips to the smoke box every hour.

4. Remove roast from grill. When cool enough to handle, shred pork by hand. Place shredded pork in a large bowl and toss with $^{1}/_{2}$ to 1 cup sauce. Serve pork on Texas toast with remaining sauce on the side.

INDOOR METHOD:
Prepare roast as directed. Place in 5-quart slow cooker. Combine apple cider and whiskey; pour over roast. Cover and cook on low-heat setting for 7 to 8 hours or on high-heat setting for 3 to 4 hours (meat should fall apart easily). Serve as directed in step 4.

North Carolina Pulled Pork Sandwiches

servings 6 **prep time** 25 minutes
grilling time 4 hours

YOU WILL NEED
Drip pan
2 cups hickory chips, soaked in water for at least 1 hour and drained
Medium bowl
2 large bowls

FOR PORK:
3^1/$_2$ pounds pork shoulder roast
   Garlic salt, *Lawry's*®
   Ground black pepper, *McCormick*®

FOR SAUCE:
1^1/$_2$ cups white vinegar, *Heinz*®
^{3}/$_4$ cup lemon-lime soda, *7UP*®
1   tablespoon Montreal steak seasoning, *McCormick*® *Grill Mates*®
2   teaspoons red pepper flakes

1   package (16-ounce) shredded cabbage, *Ready Pac*®
   Hamburger buns

1. Set up grill for indirect cooking over medium heat (no heat source under roast; see page 19).

2. Rinse pork with cold water and pat dry. Season with garlic salt and ground black pepper. Add some of the soaked wood chips to the smoke box if using a gas grill or place chips on hot coals if using charcoal. Place roast on hot grill over drip pan. Cover and cook 4 to 6 hours or until roast is very tender. If using charcoal, add 10 briquettes and a handful of soaked wood chips to coals every hour. If using a gas grill, add a handful of soaked wood chips to the smoke box every hour. Remove roast from grill.

3. Meanwhile, in a medium bowl, combine sauce ingredients; set aside. In a large bowl, toss shredded cabbage with ½ cup of sauce; set aside.

4. When cool enough to handle, shred pork by hand. Place shredded pork in a large bowl and toss with ½ to 1 cup sauce. Pile cabbage mixture and seasoned pulled pork on hamburger buns. Serve remaining sauce on the side.

INDOOR METHOD:
Prepare pork shoulder as directed. Place in 5-quart slow cooker. Pour 1 cup of lemon-lime soda over roast (in addition to soda called for in sauce mixture). Cover and cook on low-heat setting for 7 to 8 hours or high-heat setting for 3 to 4 hours (roast should fall apart easily). Continue as directed in step 3.

Red-Eye Rubbed
Pork Chops

servings 4 **prep time** 5 minutes
curing time 1 hour **standing time** 20 minutes
grilling time 10 minutes

The minute these pork chops hit the grill, their scent will wake up your taste buds. A coffee crust as rich and dark as espresso with a spoonful of brown sugar adds a bittersweet texture to juicy, succulent pork. Serve with a side of BBQ sauce for a spunky finish.

YOU WILL NEED
Small bowl
Large zip-top bag
Oil

2   tablespoons ground coffee, *Folgers®*
2   tablespoons Sandra's Sassy All-Purpose Rub (page 19)
1   tablespoon packed brown sugar
1   tablespoon poultry seasoning, *McCormick®*
1½ pounds boneless pork loin chops, thick cut
     Sandra's Signature Barbecue Sauce (page 19)

1. In a small bowl, combine coffee, All-Purpose Rub, brown sugar, and poultry seasoning; set aside.

2. Rinse pork chops and pat dry. Rub 1 to 2 times with rub mixture. Place in a zip-top bag and seal. Cure in refrigerator for at least 1 hour.

3. Set up grill for direct cooking over medium heat (see page 19). Oil grate when ready to start cooking. Remove chops from refrigerator; let stand at room temperature about 20 minutes.

4. Place chops on hot, oiled grill. Cook 5 to 6 minutes per side or until slightly pink in the centers and juices run clear (160 degrees F).

5. Serve hot with Barbecue Sauce on the side.

INDOOR METHOD:
Prepare chops as directed. Preheat broiler. Place chops on foil-lined sheet pan or broiler pan. Place 4 to 6 inches from heat source; cook for 5 minutes per side or until slightly pink in the centers and juices run clear. Serve as directed.

Pork Chops with Alabama White Sauce

servings 4 prep time 10 minutes
grilling time 12 minutes

YOU WILL NEED
Oil
Small bowl

FOR SAUCE:
3/4   cup mayonnaise, *Best Foods®* or *Hellmann's®*
1/2   cup apple cider vinegar, *Heinz®*
2   teaspoons prepared horseradish, *Morehouse®*
1   teaspoon lemon juice, *ReaLemon®*
1/2   teaspoon salt
1/4   teaspoon ground black pepper, *McCormick®*

FOR CHOPS:
1 1/2 **pounds bone-in pork chops, 1/2 inch thick**
      Garlic salt, *Lawry's®*
      Ground black pepper

INDOOR METHOD:
Prepare sauce and chops as directed. In a large skillet, heat 3 tablespoons olive oil over medium-high heat. Place chops in skillet. Cook about 4 minutes per side or until golden brown and slightly pink in the center (160 degrees F). Serve as directed.

1. Set up grill for direct cooking over medium heat (see page 19). Oil grate when ready to start cooking.

2. For sauce, in a bowl, combine mayonnaise, vinegar, horseradish, lemon juice, salt, and the 1/4 teaspoon black pepper; set aside.

3. Rinse pork chops with cold water and pat dry. Season both sides of chops with garlic salt and pepper.

4. Place chops on hot, oiled grill. Cook for 6 to 7 minutes per side or until slightly pink in the center and juices run clear (160 degrees F).

5. Serve chops with sauce.

Mai Tai Pork Skewers

servings 4 **prep time** 15 minutes
marinating time 1 hour **grilling time** 16 minutes

This spirited dish takes its festive flavor straight from the bar. Pork tenderloins are shaken—not stirred—with mai tai mix and rum, then garnished with pineapple and onions, and given a twist on the grill. Served straight up—or on a bed of rice—they go down easy.

YOU WILL NEED
Large zip-top bag
Oil
Eight 10-inch metal skewers

$1^1/2$ **pounds pork tenderloins, trimmed, cut into 1-inch pieces**
1   **cup mai tai mix,** *Trader Vic's®*
$^1/2$ **cup canola oil,** *Wesson®*
$^1/3$ **cup dark rum,** *Myers's®*
1   **teaspoon salt**
1   **teaspoon ground black pepper,** *McCormick®*
1   **teaspoon crushed garlic,** *Christopher Ranch®*
12   **ounces refrigerated pineapple wedges, cut into 1-inch pieces,** *Dole®*
1   **large red onion, cut into 1-inch pieces**

INDOOR METHOD:
Prepare skewers as directed. Preheat broiler. Place the skewers on foil-lined sheet pan or broiler pan. Place the skewers 6 inches from heat source. Cook 12 to 20 minutes, about 3 to 5 minutes per side, or until pork is cooked through. Serve hot.

1. In a large zip-top bag, place pork tenderloin pieces, mai tai mix, oil, rum, salt, pepper, and garlic. Mix thoroughly. Squeeze air out of bag and seal. Marinate in refrigerator for 1 to 3 hours.

2. Set up grill for direct cooking over medium heat (see page 19). Oil grate when ready to start cooking.

3. Remove pork pieces from marinade; discard marinade. Alternately thread pork, pineapple, and onions onto skewers.

4. Place on hot, oiled grill. Cook 16 to 24 minutes, about 4 to 6 minutes per side, or until pork is cooked through. Remove from grill. Serve hot.

Cuban Mojo Pork Sandwiches

servings 4 **prep time** 20 minutes
marinating time 1 hour **standing time** 20 minutes
grilling time 4 minutes

YOU WILL NEED
  Waxed paper
  Large zip-top bag
  Small bowl
  Oil

1	**1^{1}/$_{2}$-pound pork tenderloin, trimmed**
^{1}/$_{2}$	**cup lime juice, *ReaLime*®**
^{1}/$_{2}$	**cup extra-virgin olive oil, *Bertolli*®**
2	**tablespoons frozen orange juice concentrate, *Minute Maid*®**
1	**tablespoon salt-free Mexican seasoning, *Spice Hunter*®**
	Butter
	French rolls, split in half and toasted
4	**ounces deli ham, thinly sliced**
4	**ounces sliced Swiss cheese**
	Pickle slices (optional)

1. Cut tenderloin into 1-inch-thick slices. Place between sheets of waxed paper and pound to ^{1}/$_{4}$-inch thickness. Place tenderloin slices in zip-top bag; set aside.

2. In a bowl, stir together lime juice, oil, orange juice concentrate, and Mexican seasoning. Pour into zip-top bag with the tenderloin slices. Squeeze out air and seal. Gently massage bag to make sure all slices of pork are coated. Marinate in refrigerate 1 to 3 hours.

3. Set up grill for direct cooking over medium heat (see page 19). Oil grate when ready to start cooking.

4. Remove pork from refrigerator; let stand at room temperature about 20 minutes. Remove from marinade; discard marinade.

5. Place pork on hot, oiled grill. Cook for 2 to 3 minutes per side or until pork is cooked through.

6. Serve hot on toasted, buttered French rolls with ham, Swiss cheese, and pickle slices (optional).

INDOOR METHOD:
Prepare tenderloin as directed. Preheat boiler. Place tenderloin slices on foil-lined sheet pan or broiler pan. Place 4 to 6 inches from heat source. Cook 3 to 5 minutes per side or until pork is cooked through. Serve as directed.

Balsamic-Mustard Pork Loin

servings 4 **prep time** 10 minutes
marinating time 6 hours
standing time 40 minutes **grilling time** 1 hour

YOU WILL NEED
  Large zip-top bag
  Drip pan
  Meat thermometer

1	**3-pound pork loin**
3	**tablespoons Dijon mustard,** *Grey Poupon*®
¹⁄₄	**cup balsamic vinaigrette,** *Newman's Own*®
2	**tablespoons honey,** *Sue Bee*®
2	**tablespoons garlic and herb salad dressing mix,** *Good Seasons*®
	Fresh thyme sprigs (optional)

INDOOR METHOD:
Prepare pork loin as directed. Preheat oven to 450 degrees F. Remove pork loin from marinade; discard marinade. Place loin on a rack in a roasting pan. Place in oven and immediately reduce heat to 325 degrees F. Roast for 1¼ hours to 1½ hours (about 25 minutes per pound) or until internal temperature reaches 165 degrees F. Remove from oven and tent with foil. Let stand 10 minutes before slicing (internal temperature will rise another 5 degrees). Serve as directed.

1. Rinse pork loin and pat dry. Place in zip-top bag; add remaining ingredients, except thyme. Squeeze air out of bag and seal. Gently massage bag to thoroughly combine ingredients. Marinate in refrigerator for 6 to 12 hours.

2. Set up grill for indirect cooking over medium heat (no heat source under pork; see page 19).

3. Remove pork loin from refrigerator; let stand at room temperature about 30 minutes. Remove from marinade; discard marinade.

4. Place pork on hot grill above drip pan. Cover grill. Cook 1 to 1¹⁄₂ hours or until internal temperature reaches 165 degrees F. If using charcoal grill, add 10 briquettes to each pile of coals after an hour.

5. Remove from grill and let stand 10 minutes before slicing. Garnish with fresh thyme sprigs (optional) and serve hot.

NOTE: Leftover pork makes great sandwiches!

Black Jack
Lamb Rack

servings 6 **prep time** 10 minutes **cooking time** 25 minutes
grilling time 20 minutes **standing time** 10 minutes

What was once refreshment for the chef becomes a treat for the entire table. The secret to a tasty rack of lamb is a little tipple of Jack Daniel's® in the sauce. Mixed in moderation with molasses and steak sauce, it makes every bite tender.

YOU WILL NEED
Oil
Small saucepan
Meat thermometer

FOR SAUCE:
1   cup whiskey, *Jack Daniel's*®
1   cup steak sauce, *Lea & Perrins*®
½   cup molasses, *Grandma's*®

FOR LAMB RACKS:
2   racks of lamb
1   tablespoon garlic salt, *Lawry's*®
2   teaspoons ground black pepper, *McCormick*®

Steamed snow peas (optional)

INDOOR METHOD:
Preheat oven to 425 degrees F. Prepare racks of lamb as directed. Place racks, meat sides down, on foil-lined sheet pan. Roast for 20 to 30 minutes or until internal temperature reaches 135 to 140 degrees F for medium. Baste with sauce every 10 minutes. Transfer racks to cutting board and tent with aluminum foil. Let stand 10 minutes. Serve as directed.

1. Set up grill for direct cooking over medium-high heat (see page 19). Oil grate when ready to start cooking.

2. For sauce, in a small saucepan, combine whiskey, steak sauce, and molasses. Bring to boil. Reduce heat and simmer for 20 minutes. Remove from heat; set aside.

3. Season racks of lamb with garlic salt and pepper. Place racks, meat sides down, on hot, oiled grill. Cook for 10 to 12 minutes. Turn and baste lamb racks with sauce. Continue cooking for another 10 to 12 minutes or until internal temperature reaches 135 to 140 degrees F for medium.*

4. Remove from grill and let stand 10 minutes. Meanwhile, reheat sauce to boiling. Cut racks of lamb into portion-size chops. Serve cut chops with steamed snow peas (optional) and sauce on the side.

***TIP:** If bones start to burn on the grill, fold a piece of aluminum foil over the ends.

Greek Stuffed Leg of Lamb

servings 12 **prep time** 25 minutes
grilling time 1 ½ hours
standing time 10 minutes

YOU WILL NEED
Drip pan
Medium bowl
Butcher's twine
Meat thermometer

FOR GREEK FILLING:
2   packages (10 ounces each) frozen chopped spinach, thawed, *Green Giant*®
1   package (6-ounce) crumbled feta cheese, *Athenos*®
2   tablespoons slivered almonds, *Planters*®
2   tablespoons lemon olive oil, *O Olive Oil*®
½   teaspoon red pepper flakes

FOR LAMB:
4½ pounds boneless leg of lamb, butterflied
    Garlic salt, *Lawry's*®
    Lemon pepper, *Lawry's*®
    Greek seasoning, *Spice Islands*®

    Fresh sprigs of oregano (optional)

1. Set up grill for indirect cooking over medium heat (no heat source under lamb; see page 19).

2. For Greek Filling, squeeze excess water from thawed spinach and place in medium bowl. Add remaining filling ingredients and stir to combine; set aside.

3. Remove boneless leg of lamb from netting. Rinse with water and pat dry. Lay out lamb on cutting board, opened up. With a sharp knife, butterfly open parts of lamb that are more than 1 inch thick. Season lamb with garlic salt, lemon pepper, and Greek seasoning. Evenly distribute filling mixture over the surface of lamb. Carefully roll lamb into a spiral; secure with butcher's twine. Season outside of lamb with more garlic salt, lemon pepper, and Greek seasoning.

4. Place lamb on hot grill over drip pan. Cover grill. Cook 1½ to 2 hours or until internal temperature reaches 145 degrees F for medium. If using charcoal, add 10 briquettes to each pile of coals after an hour.

5. Remove from grill and let stand 10 minutes. Slice lamb and garnish with sprigs of oregano (optional). Serve hot.

INDOOR METHOD:
Prepare lamb as directed. Preheat oven to 450 degrees F. Place lamb on a rack set in a foil-lined roasting pan. Place in oven; after 10 minutes, reduce heat to 350 degrees F. Roast for 1 to 1¼ hours or until internal temperature reaches 145 degrees F for medium. Remove from oven; tent with foil. Let stand 10 minutes; slice. Serve as directed.

Fish and Seafood

On days when you want a lighter meal, seafood is a grill's best friend. I grew up in the Pacific Northwest, where the catch of the day was dinner. The ocean (by way of the grocery) offers everything you need to grill for a seafaring feast, from thick ahi steaks to swordfish and snapper. Stylish presentations add a regional flair—bacon-grilled trout served Cajun-style, catfish gone Mexican with black beans and salsa, or tuna given French flair in a salad niçoise. Encrusted with herbs or dressed up for company with an elegant sauce, seafood is an instant meal maker for any season and any occasion. Just flop it on the grill, and you'll be hooked!

The Recipes

Napa Valley Wine Planked Salmon

servings 4 **prep time** 10 minutes
marinating time 30 minutes **grilling time** 8 minutes

Cooking fish on a cedar plank is a Native American custom, updated here by soaking the plank in red wine. As the wood heats up, its aromatic oils are mulled with red wine, permeating the salmon to enhance its natural sweetness. A champagne vinaigrette marinade amplifies the taste, making the fish bubble with flavor.

YOU WILL NEED
Large zip-top bag
Cedar or alder grilling plank, soaked in equal parts of red wine and water for at least 2 hours and drained

1	**1 1/4-pound salmon fillet**
1	**cup champagne vinaigrette, *Girard's*®**
2	**tablespoons Dijon mustard, *Grey Poupon*®**
	Salt and ground black pepper
1/3	**cup finely chopped fresh herbs (such as parsley, oregano, basil, marjoram)**

1. In a large zip-top bag, combine salmon, champagne vinaigrette, and mustard. Squeeze air out of bag and seal. Gently massage bag to coat fillet. Marinate in refrigerator for 30 minutes.

2. Set up grill for direct cooking over medium-high heat (see page 19).

3. Remove salmon from marinade; discard marinade. Place on wine-soaked plank. Season salmon with salt and pepper; cover generously with herbs.

4. Place planked salmon on grill. Cover grill; cook for 8 to 12 minutes or until salmon is pale pink and flakes easily when tested with a fork. Remove from grill and serve hot.

INDOOR METHOD:
Prepare salmon as directed. Preheat oven to 450 degrees F. Remove salmon fillets from marinade; discard marinade. Place salmon on a foil-lined sheet pan. Season with salt and pepper; cover with herbs. Bake for 8 to 10 minutes or until salmon is pale pink and flakes easily when tested with a fork. Remove from oven; tent with foil and let stand for 5 minutes. Serve as directed.

Grilled Tuna Niçoise

servings 4 prep time 25 minutes marinating time 1 hour
standing time 20 minutes grilling time 8 minutes

YOU WILL NEED
Medium bowl
Toothpicks
Large zip-top bag
Oil

4	**tuna steaks, 1 inch thick**
1/3	**cup olive bruschetta topping,** * *Delallo®*
1	**tablespoon capers, drained,** *Star®*
1	**teaspoon crushed garlic,** *Christopher Ranch®*
1 1/2	**cups Italian dressing,** *Newman's Own®*
4	**cups mixed salad greens,** *Fresh Express®*
2	**hard-cooked eggs, sliced**
1	**cup frozen French-cut green beans, thawed and drained**
1	**tomato, cut into wedges**
1	**can (15-ounce) sliced potatoes**
	Fresh basil sprigs (optional)

1. Using a sharp knife, cut a pocket into the side of each tuna steak; set aside. In a medium bowl, combine olive bruschetta topping, capers, and garlic. Set aside 1 tablespoon of olive mixture. Stuff remaining olive mixture into pockets in tuna steaks and secure openings with toothpicks.

2. Place stuffed tuna steaks in a large zip-top bag; cover with Italian dressing. Squeeze air out of bag and seal. Marinate in refrigerator 1 to 3 hours.

3. Set up grill for direct cooking over medium heat (see page 19). Oil grate when ready to start cooking. Remove tuna steaks from marinade; discard marinade. Let tuna steaks stand at room temperature about 20 minutes.

4. Place tuna on hot, oiled grill. Cook 8 to 12 minutes or until fish flakes easily when tested with a fork, turning once. (Be careful not to overcook because tuna will dry out quickly.) Remove tuna from grill; set aside.

5. Divide mixed salad greens among four plates. Remove toothpicks from tuna steaks. Place a grilled tuna steak on top of each salad. Top each tuna steak with some of remaining olive mixture. Around the edges of the plates, arrange egg slices, green beans, tomato wedges, and sliced potatoes. Garnish with fresh basil sprigs (optional).

INDOOR METHOD:
Preheat oven to 400 degrees F. Prepare tuna steaks as directed. In a large ovenproof skillet, heat 2 tablespoons olive oil over medium-high heat. Add stuffed tuna steaks to skillet and sear until brown. Carefully turn over each steak and sear on other side. Place ovenproof skillet in oven and bake for 5 to 10 minutes or until tuna flakes easily when tested with a fork. Serve as directed.

*NOTE: If olive bruschetta topping is not available, substitute purchased olive tapenade or chopped black olives.

Caesar Swordfish Packets

servings 4 prep time 15 minutes
marinating time 30 minutes
grilling time 8 minutes

Big taste often comes in small packets. Grilling swordfish in foil is an easier version of the French method of *en papillote* (in paper)—enshrining seasoned fish and vegetables in a pouch to intensify flavor. This rendition partners a Caesar dressing marinade with a grilled salad of onions, lemons, and peppery croutons.

YOU WILL NEED
Large zip-top bag
Heavy-duty aluminum foil

4	swordfish steaks, about ¾ inch thick
1½	cups Caesar salad dressing, *Newman's Own®*
	Salt and ground black pepper
1	onion, sliced
1	lemon, sliced
½	cup Caesar croutons, *Pepperidge Farms®*

1. In a large zip-top bag, combine swordfish steaks and salad dressing. Squeeze air out of bag and seal. Marinate in refrigerator for 30 minutes.

2. Set up grill for direct cooking over medium heat (see page 19).

3. Remove fish from marinade, reserving marinade. Place each fish steak on a sheet of heavy-duty aluminum foil. Season with salt and pepper. Top fish with onion slices, lemon slices, and croutons. Sprinkle 1 tablespoon of the reserved marinade over each piece of fish. Seal foil packets by crimping edges, leaving a little room for steam.

4. Place packets on hot grill. Cook 8 to 10 minutes or until swordfish flakes easily when tested with a fork. Remove packets from grill.

5. Carefully open packets to let steam escape. Remove fish steaks from the packets; drizzle with cooking juices from the foil. Serve hot.

INDOOR METHOD:
Preheat oven to 400 degrees F. Prepare packets as directed. Place packets on sheet pan. Bake for 12 to 15 minutes or until swordfish flakes easily when tested with a fork. Serve as directed.

New Mexico Catfish with Bean Salsa

servings 4 **prep time** 10 minutes
curing time 30 minutes
grilling time 8 minutes

YOU WILL NEED
Oil
Large plate or platter
Plastic wrap
Medium bowl

1 1/4 **pounds catfish fillets**
1 **teaspoon lime juice, *ReaLime*®**
2 **tablespoons Southwest marinade mix, *McCormick® Grill Mates*®**
1 **can (15-ounce) low-sodium black beans, drained, *S&W*®**
1 **can (11-ounce) sweet and zesty mexicorn, drained, *Green Giant*®**
1 **can (10-ounce) diced tomatoes with lime juice and cilantro, drained, *Ro-Tel*®**
2 **teaspoons lime juice, *ReaLime*®**
1/2 **teaspoon salt**
Lime slices (optional)
Paprika (optional)

1. Set up grill for direct cooking over medium heat (see page 19). Oil grate when ready to start cooking.

2. Place fillets on a large plate. Sprinkle catfish with the 1 teaspoon lime juice. Pat Southwest marinade mix onto both sides of fish. Cover with plastic wrap; cure in refrigerator for 30 minutes.

3. Meanwhile, in a medium bowl, combine black beans, mexicorn, and diced tomatoes. Add the 2 teaspoons lime juice and the salt; set aside.

4. Place fillets on hot, oiled grill. Cook for 4 to 6 minutes per side or until fish flakes easily when tested with a fork. Remove fish from grill.

5. Garnish catfish fillets with lime slices and sprinkle with paprika (optional). Serve hot on salsa.

INDOOR METHOD:
Prepare catfish as directed. In a large skillet, melt 2 tablespoons of unsalted butter over high heat. Place fillets in skillet; fry about 3 minutes per side or until the fish flakes easily when tested with a fork. Transfer to a serving platter. Serve as directed.

Bacon-Grilled Cajun Trout

servings 4   prep time 25 minutes
marinating time 30 minutes   cooking time 5 minutes
grilling time 15 minutes

In Cajun country, they call it mojo—magic as mysterious as it is spiritual. Enchantingly earthy yet elegant, this smoked trout grills up a little mojo of its own. Chargrilled, but not blackened, it calls on a jazzy pepper marinade to set the flavor and wrapping the fish in bacon for a flamboyant finish.

YOU WILL NEED
Oil
Large zip-top bag
Small saucepan
Butcher's twine (twelve 6- to 8-inch-long pieces)
Sheet pan

1	**bottle (16-ounce) New Orleans Cajun marinade, *A.1.® Steakhouse***
4	**whole trout (1 pound each), cleaned, with heads and tails removed**
1	**can (14.5-ounce) diced tomatoes with green pepper, celery, and onion, *Hunt's®***
1/4	**cup real crumbled bacon, *Hormel®***
1	**tablespoon Cajun seasoning, *McCormick®***
1/4	**teaspoon liquid smoke, *Wright's®***
8	**slices thick-cut bacon, *Oscar Mayer®***

1. Set up grill for direct cooking over medium heat (see page 19). Oil grate when ready to start cooking.

2. Set aside 1/4 cup of the marinade. Place trout in a large zip-top bag; cover with remaining marinade. Squeeze air out of bag and seal. Marinate in refrigerator for 30 minutes.

3. In a small saucepan, combine the reserved 1/4 cup marinade, tomatoes, crumbled bacon, Cajun seasoning, and liquid smoke. Bring to a boil. Reduce heat and simmer for 5 minutes; set aside.

4. Lay 3 pieces of butcher's twine horizontally on a sheet pan, evenly spaced. Lay 1 slice of bacon vertically on top of butcher's twine. Remove fish from marinade; discard marinade. Place one trout on top of bacon slice. Top fish with another slice of bacon. Tie each piece of twine so that you have 3 knots securely holding the bacon in place. Repeat with remaining twine, trout, and bacon slices.

5. Place trout on hot, oiled grill. Cook for 15 to 18 minutes or until fish flakes easily when tested with a fork, turning every 3 to 4 minutes. (Watch for flare-ups from bacon slices.) Remove from grill. Untie and remove twine from fish. Top with tomato-bacon mixture and serve warm.

INDOOR METHOD:
Prepare trout as directed. Preheat oven to 450 degrees F. Place prepared trout on foil-lined sheet pan. Bake for 30 minutes or until fish flakes easily when tested with a fork. Serve as directed.

Halibut Tacos with Peach Salsa

servings 4   **prep time** 15 minutes
curing time 30 minutes   **grilling time** 8 minutes
standing time 10 minutes

Fish tacos are Mexico's Baja Peninsula's claim to fame. From humble beginnings comes this suave upgrade that combines inexpensive grilled halibut with coolly sophisticated peach salsa. Rolled in corn tortillas with a sprinkling of coleslaw, these tacos add a coastal ambiance to any occasion.

YOU WILL NEED
Oil
Plate
Plastic wrap
Medium bowl

1	**pound halibut**
1	**packet (1-ounce) hot taco seasoning, *Lawry's*®**
2	**cups mild chunky salsa, *Newman's Own*®**
1	**cup frozen peach slices, chopped* and thawed, *Dole*®**
1	**teaspoon ground allspice, *McCormick*®**
8	**supersize yellow corn tortillas, warmed, *Mission*®**
1	**package (8-ounce) coleslaw mix, *Ready Pac*®**

INDOOR METHOD:
Prepare halibut as directed. Preheat oven to 400 degrees F. Heat a large heavy skillet (preferably cast-iron) over medium-high heat until very hot. (Turn stove fan/vent on high.) Add 1 tablespoon canola oil and swirl to coat bottom of the skillet. Place fillets in skillet and cook 2 to 3 minutes per side or until very brown and fish flakes easily when tested with a fork. Remove from the skillet. Let stand for 10 minutes. Serve as directed.

1. Set up grill for direct cooking over medium heat (see page 19). Oil grate when ready to start cooking.

2. Place halibut on a plate; rub with taco seasoning. Cover with plastic wrap. Cure in the refrigerator for 30 minutes.

3. Place halibut on hot, oiled grill. Cover grill. Cook 4 minutes per side or until fish flakes easily when tested with a fork. Remove from grill. Let stand 10 minutes.

4. Meanwhile, in a medium bowl, combine salsa, peaches, and allspice.

5. Cut halibut into bite-size pieces. Place halibut pieces in warmed tortillas. Top with salsa and coleslaw mix. Serve warm.

*TIP: It is easier to chop frozen fruit while it is still frozen.

Striped Bass Monterey

servings 4 prep time 15 minutes
marinating time 30 minutes
standing time 20 minutes grilling time 8 minutes

YOU WILL NEED
Large zip-top bag
Oil
Microwave-safe bowl

1¹/₂ pounds striped bass fillets

FOR MARINADE:
2   cups white wine
1¹/₂ cups tomato juice, *Campbell's*®
2   tablespoons orange juice concentrate, *Minute Maid*®
2   tablespoons crushed garlic, *Christopher Ranch*®

FOR TOPPING:
1   bag (14-ounce) frozen pepper strips, *C&W*®
1   cup frozen chopped onion, *C&W*®
1   tablespoon extra-virgin olive oil, *Bertolli*®
2   teaspoons crushed garlic, *Christopher Ranch*®
¹/₂ teaspoon salt
¹/₄ teaspoon ground black pepper, *McCormick*®

INDOOR METHOD:
Prepare fish as directed. Remove fish from marinade; discard marinade. Pat fish dry with paper towels; set aside. In a large skillet, heat 2 tablespoons olive oil over medium-high heat. When oil is hot, add fish fillets; fry 2 to 3 minutes per side or until fish flakes easily when tested with a fork. Transfer fish to plate; set aside. Add 1 tablespoon olive oil to pan. When hot, add topping ingredients. Cook for 5 minutes or until vegetables are heated through. Reduce heat to low and add cooked fish fillets to skillet. Cover and heat through for 5 to 10 minutes. Serve as directed.

1. Rinse fish under cold water and pat dry. Place in large zip-top bag. Add white wine, tomato juice, orange juice concentrate, and garlic. Squeeze air out of bag and seal. Gently massage bag to combine ingredients. Marinate in refrigerator for 30 minutes to 2 hours.

2. Set up grill for direct cooking over medium heat (see page 19). Oil grate when ready to start cooking.

3. Remove fish from refrigerator; let stand at room temperature about 20 minutes. Remove fish from marinade and discard marinade.

4. In a microwave-safe bowl, combine pepper strips, onion, olive oil, garlic, salt, and pepper. Cover and cook on high setting (100% power) in microwave oven for 5 minutes; set aside.

5. Place fillets, flesh sides down, on hot, oiled grill. Cook for 4 to 5 minutes. Turn fish; cook for another 4 to 5 minutes or until fish flakes easily when tested with a fork. Remove from grill.

6. Top fillets with onion-pepper strip mixture. Serve hot.

Grilled Snapper with Vera Cruz Salsa

servings 4 **prep time** 10 minutes
grilling time 8 minutes

Red snapper comes from warm, tropical climates, where spicy foods are the norm. So do as the natives do and season it with strong flavors. An unfussy rub of Mexican seasonings and tequila lime salsa is all you need to bring out the fish's naturally nutty flavor.

YOU WILL NEED
Oil
Medium bowl

1½ **pounds snapper fillets**
2 **tablespoons Mexican seasoning, *McCormick*®**
 Salt and ground black pepper

FOR SALSA:
1 **cup tequila lime salsa, *Newman's Own*®**
½ **cup sliced Spanish olives, drained, *Star*®**
1 **tablespoon capers, drained, *Star*®**
¼ **teaspoon crushed garlic, *Christopher Ranch*®**

INDOOR METHOD:
Prepare snapper as directed. Place fillets on lightly oiled foil-lined sheet pan or broiler pan; set aside while preparing salsa. Preheat broiler. Place fillets 4 inches from heat source. Cook for 3 to 4 minutes per side or until fish flakes easily when tested with a fork. Remove from the oven. Serve as directed.

1. Set up grill for direct cooking over medium heat (see page 19). Oil grate when ready to start cooking.

2. Rinse fillets with cold water and pat dry. Season with Mexican seasoning, salt, and pepper. Set aside while preparing salsa.

3. In a medium bowl, combine salsa, Spanish olives, capers, and garlic; set aside.

4. Place fillets, flesh sides down, on hot, oiled grill. Cook for 4 to 5 minutes. Turn fish and cook another 4 to 5 minutes or until fish flakes easily when tested with a fork. Remove from grill.

5. Top with salsa. Serve hot.

Pineapple
Seafood Bowls

servings 6 **prep time** 30 minutes
grilling time 20 minutes

YOU WILL NEED
Oil
Heavy-duty aluminum foil
Medium bowl

3	**large fresh pineapples**
1	**can (13.5-ounce) lite coconut milk, *Taste of Thai*®**
1/2	**cup chopped fresh cilantro**
2	**teaspoons Thai seasoning, *Spice Islands*®**
1	**pound cod, cut into 1-inch pieces**
8	**ounces bay scallops, cleaned**
8	**ounces rock shrimp, cleaned**
	Fresh cilantro (optional)

1. Set up grill for direct cooking over medium heat (see page 19). Oil grate when ready to start cooking.

2. Cut pineapples in half. Scoop the flesh from each pineapple to create a bowl (leave bottom portion in each pineapple bowl to hold coconut milk mixture). Reserve the removed pineapple flesh. Wrap bottoms of the pineapple bowls with a double layer of heavy-duty foil.

3. Cut the reserved pineapple flesh into bite-size pieces (discard the hard core section). In a medium bowl, combine pineapple, coconut milk, cilantro, and Thai seasoning. Fill each pineapple bowl halfway full of coconut milk mixture.

4. Place pineapple bowls on hot, oiled grill. Cover grill. Cook for 15 to 20 minutes or until the coconut milk mixture begins to simmer.

5. Once the coconut milk mixture simmers, divide seafood among pineapple bowls. Cover grill; cook for 5 minutes or until seafood is opaque and cooked through.

6. Remove seafood bowls from grill; carefully remove foil. Garnish with fresh cilantro (optional) and serve hot.

INDOOR METHOD:
Preheat oven to 400 degrees F. Prepare and fill pineapple bowls as directed. Place bowls on foil-lined sheet pan. Bake until broth begins to simmer (about 25 to 30 minutes). Add seafood to bowls and continue baking about 5 to 10 minutes or until seafood is opaque and cooked through. Serve as directed.

Shrimp and Mango Brochettes

servings 4 **prep time** 15 minutes
marinating time 30 minutes
standing time 20 minutes **grilling time** 4 minutes

YOU WILL NEED
Oil
12-inch wood skewers, soaked in water at least 1 hour and drained
Deep rectangular dish, large enough to hold brochettes
Serving platter

1	**pound medium shrimp, peeled and deveined**
12	**ounces cherry tomatoes, *Nature Sweet*®**
1	**bag (16-ounce) frozen mango chunks, *Dole*®**
1	**bottle (16-ounce) honey teriyaki with sesame marinade, *KC Masterpiece*®**
1	**scallion (green onion), chopped**
1	**tablespoon sesame seeds**
	Bias-sliced scallion (green onion) (optional)
	Halved cherry tomatoes (optional)

1. Set up grill for direct cooking over medium-high heat (see page 19). Oil grate when ready to start cooking.

2. Insert presoaked skewer through center of a shrimp, cherry tomato, and mango chunk.* Repeat layers 3 times (about 3 of each will fit on each skewer). Place brochettes in a deep dish. Pour honey teriyaki marinade over top and sprinkle with chopped scallion. Marinate in the refrigerator for 30 minutes.

3. Remove brochettes from refrigerator. Remove skewers from marinade; discard marinade. Let brochettes stand at room temperature about 20 minutes.

4. Place skewers about 1 inch apart on grill. Cook 2 to 3 minutes per side or until shrimp is opaque and cooked through. Remove from grill.

5. Transfer brochettes to a serving platter. Sprinkle with sesame seeds. Garnish with bias-sliced scallion and halved cherry tomatoes (optional). Serve hot.

*****NOTE:** For appetizer servings, use 4-inch skewers (see photo, left). Thread each skewer with only 1 piece of each ingredient.

INDOOR METHOD:
Prepare skewers as directed. Preheat boiler. Lay skewers out on foil-lined sheet pan or broiler pan. Place skewers 4 to 6 inches from heat source. Cook for 3 minutes. Turn; continue cooking for 3 to 4 minutes more or until shrimp is opaque and cooked through. Serve as directed.

Spicy Peel and Eat Shrimp with Chipotle Cocktail Sauce

servings 4   **prep time** 20 minutes
marinating time 30 minutes
grilling time 4 minutes
chilling time 2 hours

YOU WILL NEED
Oil
Large zip-top bag
Blender
Medium bowl
Large bowl with ice
Platter

FOR SHRIMP:
2   pounds large shrimp (with shells and legs)
1   bottle (12-ounce) chipotle marinade, *Lawry's*®
½   cup chopped fresh cilantro leaves

FOR COCKTAIL SAUCE:
1   jar (16-ounce) chipotle salsa, *Pace*®
1   cup cocktail sauce, *Heinz*®
2   teaspoons chipotle hot sauce, *Tabasco*®
Lemon wedges (optional)
Fresh cilantro leaf (optional)

1. Set up grill for direct cooking over medium-high heat (see page 19). Oil grate when ready to start cooking.

2. In a large zip-top bag, combine shrimp, chipotle marinade, and cilantro. Squeeze air out of bag and seal. Gently massage bag to combine ingredients. Marinate in refrigerator for 30 minutes.

3. In a blender, combine, salsa, cocktail sauce, and hot sauce. Blend until smooth. Transfer to a medium bowl; cover and refrigerate until needed.

4. Remove shrimp from the refrigerator. Remove shrimp from marinade; discard marinade.

5. Place shrimp on hot, oiled grill. Cook about 2 to 3 minutes per side or until shrimp are opaque and cooked through. Do not overcook. Remove shrimp and transfer to a large bowl filled with ice. Refrigerate shrimp about 2 hours or until completely chilled.

6. Place cold shrimp on a platter. Garnish with lemon wedges and cilantro sprig (optional). Serve cocktail sauce on the side.*

***NOTE:** Don't forget a bowl for peeled shells!

INDOOR METHOD:
Prepare shrimp as directed. Preheat broiler. Place shrimp on foil-lined sheet pan or broiler pan. Place about 4 inches from heat source. Cook for 4 minutes. Turn and cook another 4 minutes or until shrimp is opaque and cooked through. Chill; serve as directed.

Piña Colada Scallop Brochettes

servings 4 **prep time** 20 minutes
marinating time 30 minutes **grilling time** 8 minutes

YOU WILL NEED
Large zip-top bag
Oil
Four 12-inch wood or metal skewers (if using wood skewers, soak in water at least 2 hours and drain)

12	large sea scallops
1	can (10-ounce) frozen piña colada mix, thawed, *Bacardi®*
1/2	cup light rum, *Bacardi®*
1	teaspoon ground black pepper, *McCormick®*
1	teaspoon crushed garlic, *Christopher Ranch®*
1/2	teaspoon salt
12	ounces fresh pineapple wedges, cut into 1-inch pieces, *Dole®*
1	cup shredded coconut, toasted, *Baker's®*

1. In a large zip-top bag, combine scallops, thawed piña colada mix, rum, pepper, garlic, and salt. Squeeze air out of bag and seal. Gently massage bag to combine ingredients. Marinate in refrigerator for 30 minutes to 2 hours.

2. Set up grill for direct cooking over medium heat (see page 19). Oil grate when ready to start cooking.

3. Remove scallops from marinade; discard marinade. Alternately thread pineapple and scallops onto skewers. Skewer scallops through the sides so that the tops and bottoms are facing out (see photo, left).

4. Spread toasted coconut on a plate; set aside.

5. Place brochettes on hot, oiled grill and cook 4 to 5 minutes per side or until scallops are opaque and cooked through.

6. Remove from grill and immediately press both sides of brochettes into toasted coconut. Serve hot.

INDOOR METHOD:
Prepare brochettes as directed. Preheat broiler. Place brochettes on lightly oiled sheet pan or broiler pan. Place brochettes 4 inches from heat source. Cook for 3 to 4 minutes per side. Serve as directed.

Wasabi Ginger Soft-Shell Crabs

servings 4 **prep time** 15 minutes
marinating time 30 minutes
standing time 20 minutes **grilling time** 4 minutes

YOU WILL NEED
Oil
Large zip-top bag
Medium bowl

12 **jumbo soft-shell crabs, cleaned**
1 **bottle (12-ounce) wasabi ginger vinaigrette dressing,** *Girard's*®
2 **scallions (green onions), chopped**
2 **teaspoons lemon juice,** *ReaLemon*®
1 **teaspoon ground black pepper,** *McCormick*®
Snipped fresh chives or chopped scallion (green part only)
 (optional)
Pickled ginger (optional)
Wasabi (optional)

1. Set up grill for direct cooking over medium-high heat (see page 19). Oil grate when ready to start cooking.

2. Place cleaned soft-shell crabs in a large zip-top bag; set aside. In a medium bowl, stir to combine vinaigrette dressing, scallions, lemon juice, and pepper. Reserve 1 cup of marinade; pour remaining marinade in zip-top bag over crabs. Squeeze air out of bag and seal. Marinate in refrigerator for 30 minutes to 2 hours.

3. Remove crabs from refrigerator; let stand at room temperature about 20 minutes. Remove crabs from marinade; discard marinade.

4. Place the crabs a few inches apart on hot, oiled grill. Grill crabs for 2 to 3 minutes per side or until claws turn red. Glaze each side with reserved marinade when turning. Remove from grill. Garnish with snipped chives, pickled ginger, and wasabi (optional).

INDOOR METHOD:
Prepare soft-shell crabs as directed. In a large skillet, heat ½ inch of vegetable oil over medium-high heat. (350 to 375 degrees F). Remove crabs from marinade. Gently shake off excess; discard marinade. Dredge crabs in flour; fry 5 minutes per side or until brown. Serve as directed.

Burgers and Dogs

Summer's cookouts become fall's tailgates. I went to college in Wisconsin and discovered that grilling's even better with a chill in the air. Tailgating is dedicated to the pursuit of the perfect burger—the meat moist and juicy, the buns slapped on the grill just long enough to get them crisp and buttery brown. This chapter gives you plenty of contenders—Stuffed Chili Cheeseburgers, turkey burgers, even lamb burgers—smothered in gourmet toppings such Cognac-Mustard Sauce, Maple-Dijon Sauce, and Garlic-Mint Aïoli. There are old-fashioned franks that taste like they are straight from the street cart and sausages with beer-braised onions that will bring back memories of fall with every bite. Park yourself out back with a group of friends and a kickoff cocktail for a fantastic all-season outing.

The Recipes

Black Pepper-Crusted Burgers with Cognac-Mustard Sauce

servings 4 prep time 15 minutes
cooking time 9 minutes
grilling time 8 minutes

YOU WILL NEED
Small saucepan
Small bowl
Large bowl
Oil
Plate

FOR COGNAC-MUSTARD SAUCE:
1/2 **cup cognac (or apple cider)**
1/2 **cup Dijon mustard, *Grey Poupon*®**
2 **teaspoons chopped fresh tarragon**

FOR BLACK PEPPER-CRUSTED BURGERS:
1 1/2 **pounds ground sirloin**
1/4 **cup cognac**
1 **package (1-ounce) onion soup mix, *Lipton*®**
1/2 **cup cracked black pepper**
Kaiser rolls, toasted
Lettuce, tomato slices, and red onion slices
Relish skewers (cherry tomatoes, olives, small pickles) (optional)

1. For Cognac-Mustard Sauce, in a small saucepan over medium-high heat, bring the 1/2 cup cognac to a boil. Cook 4 to 5 minutes or until reduced by half. Remove from heat and let cool. Once cognac has cooled, transfer to small bowl; add mustard and tarragon. Stir to combine; set aside.

2. Set up grill for direct cooking over high heat (see page 19). Oil grate when ready to start cooking.

3. For Black Pepper-Crusted Burgers, in a large bowl, stir to combine ground sirloin, the 1/4 cup cognac, and the onion soup mix. Form into 4 patties* slightly larger than the rolls; set aside. Spread cracked pepper on a plate. Carefully press both sides of burgers into cracked pepper. (Cover with plastic wrap and refrigerate if not cooking immediately.)

4. Place burgers on hot, oiled grill and cook 4 to 5 minutes per side for medium (160 degrees F). To serve, place hot burgers on toasted kaiser rolls. Top with lettuce, tomato, onion, and Cognac-Mustard Sauce. Garnish with relish skewers (optional).

INDOOR METHOD:
Preheat oven to 400 degrees F. Prepare burgers as directed. Place burgers on wire rack over foil-lined sheet pan. Roast for 19 to 20 minutes for medium (160 degrees F). Serve as directed.

*TIP: Wet your hands before forming patties to prevent sticking.

Bleu Cheese and Bacon-Stuffed Burgers

servings 4 **prep time** 15 minutes
grilling time 8 minutes

YOU WILL NEED
Small bowl
Oil
Large bowl

FOR BLEU CHEESE BUTTER:
4   **tablespoons butter**
2   **tablespoons bleu cheese crumbles, *Treasure Cave*®**

FOR BACON-STUFFED BURGERS:
1$^{1}/_{2}$ **pounds lean ground beef**
$^{1}/_{2}$ **cup bleu cheese crumbles, *Treasure Cave*®**
$^{1}/_{4}$ **cup real bacon pieces, *Hormel*®**
1   **tablespoon Montreal steak seasoning, *McCormick*® *Grill Mates*®**
     Salt and ground black pepper
     Onion rolls, toasted
     Lettuce, tomato slices, and onion slices
     Avocado slices (optional)

1. For Bleu Cheese Butter, in a small bowl, mash together butter and the 2 tablespoons bleu cheese crumbles with a fork; set aside.

2. Set up grill for direct cooking over high heat (see page 19). Oil grate when ready to start cooking.

INDOOR METHOD:
Preheat broiler. Prepare burgers as directed. Place burgers on wire rack over foil-lined sheet pan or broiler pan. Place 6 inches from heat source. Cook for 4 to 5 minutes per side for medium (160 degrees F). Serve as directed.

3. For Bacon-Stuffed Burgers, in a large bowl, combine ground beef, the ½ cup bleu cheese crumbles, the bacon pieces, and the steak seasoning. Form into 4 patties* slightly larger than the rolls. (Cover with plastic wrap and refrigerate if not cooking immediately.)

4. Season burgers with salt and pepper. Place on hot, oiled grill. Cook for 4 to 5 minutes per side for medium (160 degrees F).

5. Spread toasted onion rolls with Bleu Cheese Butter. Serve hot burgers on the rolls with lettuce, tomato, onion. Top with avocado slices (optional).

***TIP:** Wet your hands before forming patties to prevent sticking.

Fiery Tex-Mex
Chipotle Cheeseburgers

servings 4 **prep time** 20 minutes
grilling time 8 minutes

YOU WILL NEED
Small bowl
Large bowl
Oil

FOR CHIPOTLE MAYONNAISE:
1 1/2 teaspoons finely chopped chipotles in adobo sauce,* *La Victoria®* (see tip, page 202)
3/4 cup mayonnaise, *Best Foods®* or *Hellmann's®*

FOR CHIPOTLE CHEESEBURGERS:
1 1/2 pounds lean ground beef
1/4 cup beer
2 tablespoons Tex-Mex chili seasoning, *McCormick®*
2 teaspoons finely chopped chipotles in adobo sauce, *La Victoria®*
   Salt and ground black pepper
4 slices sliced pepper Jack cheese, *Tillamook®*
   Hamburger buns, toasted
   Lettuce, tomato slices, and onion slices
   Sliced avocado (optional)

1. Remove chipotle peppers from can. Carefully split open and scrape out seeds. Finely chop peppers. For Chipotle Mayonnaise, in a small bowl, stir together 1 1/2 teaspoons of the chopped chipotles and the mayonnaise. Cover and refrigerate.

2. For Chipotle Cheeseburgers, in a large bowl, stir to combine ground beef, beer, chili seasoning, and 2 teaspoons of the chopped chipotles. Form into 4 patties** slightly larger than the buns. (Cover with plastic wrap and refrigerate if not cooking immediately.)

3. Set up grill for direct cooking over high heat (see page 19). Oil grate when ready to start cooking. Season burgers with salt and pepper. Place on hot, oiled grill. Cook for 4 to 5 minutes per side for medium (160 degrees F), placing cheese slices on burgers 2 to 3 minutes before burgers are done. Serve hot on toasted buns with Chipotle Mayonnaise, lettuce, tomato, and onion. Top with avocado slices (optional).

*NOTE: Chipotle chiles are smoked, dried jalapeños that are often packed in adobo sauce, a spicy dark red sauce made from tomatoes and herbs. Look for them in the Mexican foods section of grocery stores.

**TIP: Wet your hands before forming patties to prevent sticking.

INDOOR METHOD:
Prepare burgers as directed. Place burgers on wire rack over foil-lined sheet pan or broiler pan. Place 6 inches from heat source. Cook for 4 to 5 minutes per side for medium (160 degrees F), placing cheese slices on burgers 1 to 2 minutes before burgers are done. Serve as directed.

Pineapple Teriyaki Burgers

servings 4
prep time 10 minutes
grilling time 8 minutes

This laid-back Hawaiian burger brings a taste of the tropics to your backyard. Lean ground beef is given a dunk in a ginger teriyaki marinade, topped with pineapple rings, and grilled to sear in the flavor. Serve on a toasted bun to treat island fever year 'round.

YOU WILL NEED
Oil
Large bowl

1 1/2 **pounds lean ground beef**
1   **can (8-ounce) pineapple rings, drained (reserve juice),** *Dole®*
2   **tablespoons ginger teriyaki marinade mix,** *McCormick® Grill Mates®*
1   **packet (1.1-ounce) beefy onion soup mix,** *Lipton®*
    Salt and ground black pepper
4   **whole grain hamburger buns, toasted**
    Lettuce
    Grilled or raw onion slices
    Condiments (such as thousand island dressing)
    Grilled scallions (green onions) (optional)

INDOOR METHOD:
Prepare burgers as directed. Place burgers, pineapple sides up, on wire rack over foil-lined sheet pan or broiler pan. Place 6 inches from heat source. Cook for 4 to 5 minutes per side for medium (160 degrees F). Serve as directed.

1. Set up grill for direct cooking over high heat (see page 19). Oil grate when ready to start cooking.

2. In a large bowl, stir to combine ground beef, 1/4 cup of the reserved pineapple juice, teriyaki marinade mix, and onion soup mix. Form into 4 patties* slightly larger than buns. Gently press pineapple rings into tops of burgers (burgers may have to be reshaped back to size). Season burgers with salt and pepper.

3. Place burgers, pineapple sides down, on hot, oiled grill. Cook 4 to 5 minutes per side for medium (160 degrees F).

4. Serve hot on toasted buns with lettuce, grilled onion slices, and desired condiments. Garnish with grilled scallions (optional).

***TIP:** Wet your hands before forming patties to prevent sticking.

Stuffed Chili Cheeseburgers

servings 8 **prep time** 20 minutes
grilling time 8 minutes

The star of any All-American burger lineup has to be the chili cheeseburger. This favorite teams lean ground beef with a booster of chili seasoning to score big with burger fans. The sweet spot is the center, filled with Colby-Jack cracker snacks that melt into a tangy burst of cheese over the heat.

YOU WILL NEED
Medium bowl
Oil

2	**pounds extra-lean ground beef**
3	**tablespoons chili seasoning mix,** *McCormick*®
3	**tablespoons water**
16	**Colby-Jack cracker snacks,** *Sargento*®
8	**hamburger buns, toasted**
	Lettuce, tomato slices, and onion slices
	Condiments (such as ketchup and mustard)

INDOOR METHOD:
Prepare burgers as directed. Place burgers on wire rack over foil-lined sheet pan or broiler pan. Place 6 inches from heat source. Cook for 4 to 5 minutes per side for medium (160 degrees F). Serve as directed.

1. In a medium bowl, use your hands to combine ground beef, chili seasoning, and water. Divide beef mixture evenly into 8 pieces. Form each piece around 2 pieces of cheese snacks. Form patties* slightly larger than buns. (Be sure no cheese is showing.)

2. Set up grill for direct cooking over high heat (see page 19). Oil grate when ready to start cooking.

3. Place burgers on hot, oiled grill and cook for 4 to 5 minutes per side for medium (160 degrees F). Serve on toasted buns with lettuce, tomato, onion, and desired condiments.

*TIP: Wet your hands before forming patties to prevent sticking.

Cajun Pork Burgers with Spicy Remoulade Sauce

servings 4 **prep time** 15 minutes
chilling time 1 hour **grilling time** 10 minutes

YOU WILL NEED
Small bowl
Large bowl
Oil

FOR SPICY REMOULADE SAUCE:
1   cup tartar sauce, *Best Foods® or Hellmann's®*
1   tablespoon capers, chopped, *Star®*
1   teaspoon Cajun seasoning, *McCormick®*
1   teaspoon prepared horseradish, *Morehouse®*
3   or more dashes hot pepper sauce, *Tabasco®*

FOR CAJUN PORK BURGERS:
1$^1/_2$ **pounds ground pork**
1   tablespoon Cajun seasoning, *McCormick®*
2   scallions (green onions), green part only, finely chopped
1   teaspoon hot pepper sauce, *Tabasco®*
$^1/_2$ teaspoon salt
$^1/_2$ teaspoon ground black pepper
     Hamburger buns, toasted
     Shredded lettuce
     Pickle slices, tomato slices, and onion slices

1. For Spicy Remoulade Sauce, in a small bowl, combine all sauce ingredients. Cover and refrigerate for 1 hour to allow flavors to blend.

2. In a large bowl, stir to combine ground pork, Cajun seasoning, chopped scallions, the 1 teaspoon hot pepper sauce, the salt, and pepper. Form into 4 patties* slightly larger than buns. (Cover with plastic wrap and refrigerate if not cooking immediately.)

3. Set up grill for direct cooking over medium heat (see page 19). Oil grate when ready to start cooking.

4. Place burgers on hot, oiled grill and cook 5 to 6 minutes per side for medium (160 degrees F).

5. Serve burgers hot on toasted buns with remoulade sauce, shredded lettuce, pickle, tomato, and onion.

*TIP: Wet your hands before forming patties to prevent sticking.

INDOOR METHOD:
Prepare burgers as directed. In a large skillet, heat 2 tablespoons oil over medium-high heat. When oil is hot, add burgers and cook 6 to 8 minutes per side for medium (160 degrees F). Serve as directed.

Indian Aïoli Lamb Burgers

servings 4 **prep time** 15 minutes
grilling time 6 minutes

Thick, juicy meat; smokey flavor; a divine sauce—lamb burgers are everything you want in burgers, except beef. Mango chutney adds texture, while Garlic-Mint Aïoli provides a refreshing change of pace from the traditional mint jelly. It's the best burger this side of India.

YOU WILL NEED
Oil
2 medium bowls

FOR GARLIC-MINT AÏOLI:
$^1/_2$ **cup mayonnaise, *Best Foods*® or *Hellmann's*®**
3   tablespoons finely chopped fresh mint
1   teaspoon minced garlic, *Christopher Ranch*®
1   tablespoon extra-virgin olive oil, *Bertolli*®

FOR LAMB BURGERS:
1$^1/_2$ pounds ground lamb
$^1/_4$ **cup finely chopped fresh mint**
3   tablespoons mango chutney, *Sharwood's*®
1$^1/_2$ teaspoons garam masala,* *Spice Islands*®

Fresh mint sprigs (optional)

INDOOR METHOD:
Prepare burgers as directed. Place burgers on wire rack over foil-lined sheet pan or broiler pan. Place 6 inches from the heat source. Cook for 4 to 5 minutes per side for medium (160 degrees F). Serve as directed.

1. Set up grill for direct cooking over high heat (see page 19). Oil grate when ready to start cooking.

2. For Garlic-Mint Aïoli, in a medium bowl, combine mayonnaise, the 3 tablespoons chopped mint, the garlic, and olive oil; set aside.

3. For Lamb Burgers, in a medium bowl, combine lamb, the $^1/_4$ cup chopped mint, the chutney, and the garam masala. Mix thoroughly. Form mixture into four $^1/_2$-inch-thick patties.** Place patties on hot, oiled grill and cook for 3 to 4 minutes per side for medium (160 degrees F). To serve, top each burger with a spoonful of Garlic-Mint Aïoli. Garnish with fresh mint sprigs (optional).

*****NOTE:** Garam masala is a blend of aromatic spices used in Indian cooking. It can be found in the spice section of the grocery store.

******TIP:** Wet your hands before forming patties to prevent sticking.

TIP: Lamb burgers can also be served with toasted pita bread, tabbouleh, cucumbers, red onion, and/or crumbled feta cheese.

Apple Turkey Burgers with Maple-Dijon Sauce

servings 4   **prep time** 15 minutes
grilling time 10 minutes

Turkey burgers are often thought of as spa cuisine, but this one is as lush as it is lean. Made with healthful ground turkey, it's bursting with the familiar flavors of fall—crisp apples, sweet maple syrup, and brisk Dijon mustard. Flip a few on the grill whenever you're craving the heat of the harvest.

YOU WILL NEED
Oil
Small bowl
Medium bowl

FOR MAPLE-DIJON SAUCE:
$1/4$ cup mayonnaise, *Best Foods® or Hellmann's®*
2   tablespoons real maple syrup, *Springfield®*
1   tablespoon Dijon mustard, *Grey Poupon®*

FOR APPLE TURKEY BURGERS:
$1^{1}/4$ pounds ground turkey breast, *Jennie-O®*
$1/2$ cup chunky applesauce, *Mott's®*
$1/4$ cup real bacon bits, *Hormel®*
$1/2$ teaspoon poultry seasoning, *McCormick®*
$1/2$ teaspoon salt
$1/4$ teaspoon ground black pepper
    Hamburger buns, toasted
    Lettuce and tomato slices

1. Set up grill for direct cooking over medium heat (see page 19). Oil grate when ready to start cooking.

2. For Maple-Dijon Sauce, in a small bowl, combine mayonnaise, maple syrup, and Dijon mustard; set aside.

3. For Apple Turkey Burgers, in a medium bowl, mix together turkey, applesauce, bacon bits, poultry seasoning, salt, and pepper. Form into 4 patties* slightly larger than buns.

4. Place burgers on hot, oiled grill. Cook for 5 to 6 minutes per side or until no longer pink inside (170 degrees F).

5. Serve hot on toasted buns with Maple-Dijon Sauce, lettuce, and tomato.

*TIP: Wet your hands before forming patties to prevent sticking.

INDOOR METHOD:
Prepare burgers as directed. In a large skillet, heat 2 tablespoons vegetable oil over medium-high heat. When oil is hot, add burgers and cook 5 to 7 minutes per side or until no longer pink inside (170 degrees F). Serve as directed.

Fresh Tuna Burgers with Wasabi Slaw

servings 4   **prep time** 20 minutes
chilling time 1 hour   **grilling time** 5 minutes

YOU WILL NEED
2 large bowls
Plastic wrap
Food processor
Oil

FOR WASABI SLAW:
1/4   **cup Chinese chicken salad dressing, *Girard's®***
2   **tablespoons mayonnaise, *Best Foods® or Hellmann's®***
2   **teaspoons or more prepared wasabi**
2   **tablespoons finely chopped chives**
1/4   **cup finely chopped fresh cilantro**
3   **tablespoons sesame seeds**
1   **16-ounce bag 3-color slaw mix, *Fresh Express®***

FOR TUNA BURGERS:
1 1/4 **pounds tuna steaks**
1   **tablespoon finely chopped chives**
1   **tablespoon sesame seeds**
1   **tablespoon finely chopped fresh cilantro**
2   **teaspoons canola oil, *Wesson®***
1/2   **teaspoon salt**
1/4   **teaspoon ground black pepper, *McCormick®***

Fresh cilantro leaves (optional)

1. For Wasabi Slaw, in a large bowl, whisk together salad dressing, mayonnaise, and wasabi until smooth. Stir in chives, the 1/4 cup cilantro, and the 3 tablespoons sesame seeds. Add slaw mix and toss to combine. Cover with plastic wrap and refrigerate for 1 hour.

2. Set up grill for direct cooking over medium-high heat (see page 19). Oil grate when ready to start cooking. For Tuna Burgers, cut tuna into small pieces. Place in food processor and pulse until coarsely minced (do not overprocess). Transfer to a large bowl and stir in remaining ingredients. Form mixture into 4 patties.* (Cover with plastic wrap and refrigerate if not cooking immediately.)

3. Place burgers on hot, oiled grill. Cook 2 1/2 to 3 minutes per side for medium. (Be careful not to overcook because tuna dries out quickly.) Garnish with fresh cilantro leaves (optional). Serve hot with Wasabi Slaw on the side.

*TIP: Wet your hands before forming patties to prevent sticking.

INDOOR METHOD:
Prepare burgers as directed. Place burgers on foil-lined sheet pan or broiler pan. Place 6 inches from heat source. Cook for 3 to 4 minutes per side for medium. (Be careful not to overcook because tuna dries out quickly.) Serve as directed.

Wisconsin Beef and Cheddar Sausages with Beer-Braised Onions

serving 4 **prep time** 15 minutes
cooking time 20 minutes
grilling time 16 minutes

YOU WILL NEED
Oil
Cast-iron skillet

4	**tablespoons butter**
2	**red onions, thinly sliced**
1	**yellow onion, thinly sliced**
1	**bottle (12-ounce) beer**
8	**beef and cheddar sausages,** *Hillshire Farm®*
4	**sourdough sandwich rolls, toasted**
	Stone-ground mustard

INDOOR METHOD:
In a large skillet, melt butter over medium heat. Add sausages and brown 10 minutes, turning them occasionally as they brown. Remove the sausages and set aside. Add the onions and cook for 10 minutes, stirring frequently until softened. Pour beer over onions and scrape up any brown bits in the bottom of the skillet. Return the sausages to the skillet and cook over medium heat about 15 minutes or until beer has almost evaporated. Serve as directed.

1. Set up grill for direct cooking over high heat (see page 19). Oil grate when ready to start cooking.

2. Place cast-iron skillet on grill and add butter. When butter has melted, add onions. Cook about 10 minutes or until onions are softened. Add beer and cover; cook an additional 10 minutes. Remove cover from skillet and let onion mixture simmer.

3. If using a gas grill, turn heat down to medium (if using charcoal, it will probably be about medium at this point).

4. Place sausages on hot, oiled grill and cook 16 to 20 minutes, about 4 to 5 minutes per side. Remove from grill.

5. To serve, place two hot sausages on each toasted roll. Smother sausages with onions and top with mustard.

Hot Italian Sausage and Peppers with Balsamic Pepper and Olive Sauce

servings 4 **prep time** 20 minutes
grilling time 18 minutes

YOU WILL NEED
Oil
1 large bowl
1 small bowl

FOR BALSAMIC PEPPER AND OLIVE SAUCE:
$^1/_4$ **cup ketchup**
2   **tablespoons balsamic vinaigrette,** *Newman's Own*®
2   **tablespoons pepper and onion relish,** *Dickinson's*®
1   **tablespoon olive bruschetta topping,** * *Delallo*®

FOR SAUSAGE AND PEPPERS:
1   **sweet onion, thinly sliced**
3   **bell peppers (2 red and 1 green), seeded and cut into strips**
3   **tablespoons balsamic vinaigrette,** *Newman's Own*®
4   **hot Italian sausages**
4   **sourdough sandwich rolls, toasted**

INDOOR METHOD:
In a medium saucepan, simmer sausages in water about 20 minutes; drain and transfer to slow cooker. Cover with sliced onion and peppers (omit 3 tablespoons of balsamic vinaigrette). Pour Balsamic Pepper and Olive Sauce over top. Cover and cook on low-heat setting for 6 to 8 hours or on high-heat setting for 2 to 4 hours. Serve as directed.

1. Set up grill for direct cooking over medium heat (see page 19). Oil grate when ready to start cooking.

2. In a small bowl, stir to combine ketchup, the 2 tablespoons balsamic vinaigrette, the relish, and olive bruschetta topping; set aside.

3. In a large bowl, toss to combine sliced onion and peppers with the 3 tablespoons balsamic vinaigrette. Place vegetables on hot, oiled grill.** Cook about 10 minutes or until just tender (not mushy), turning often.

4. Meanwhile, place sausages on other side of hot, oiled grill and cook 18 to 20 minutes or until done (160 degrees F), turning often.

5. To serve, place hot sausages on toasted rolls. Top with grilled onions and peppers. Top with Balsamic Pepper and Olive Sauce.

*****NOTE:** If olive bruschetta topping is not available, substitute purchased olive tapenade or chopped black olives.

****TIP:** If you own a grill wok, use it to cook the vegetables on the grill. If you must put them directly on the grill, be careful not to let the vegetables fall between the grate when grilling.

Sausage and Bacon Kabobs

servings 4 **prep time** 15 minutes
grilling time 16 minutes

Shish kabobs are good-time food, deliciously up-tempo whether you're entertaining guests or the family. Generous chunks of chicken and apple sausages are sandwiched between wedges of hickory-smoked bacon and onion and pepper pieces, all basted with BBQ sauce. It's an all-in-one way to get dinner on a stick!

YOU WILL NEED
Oil
Four 12-inch bamboo or wood skewers, soaked in water for at least 1 hour and drained

4	chicken and apple sausages, *Aidells®*
6	slices center-cut bacon, cut into 1-inch pieces, *Oscar Mayer®*
1/2	red onion, cut into 1-inch pieces
1	green bell pepper, cut into 1-inch pieces
1	cup Sandra's Signature Barbecue Sauce (page 19) (plus some for dipping; optional)

INDOOR METHOD:
Preheat broiler. Prepare kabobs as directed. Place kabobs on wire rack over foil-lined sheet pan or broiler pan. Place 4 to 6 inches from heat source. Cook for 3 to 5 minutes per side. Brush with Barbecue Sauce with each turn. Serve as directed.

1. Set up grill for direct cooking over medium heat (see page 19). Oil grate when ready to start cooking.

2. Cut each sausage crosswise into 5 pieces. Thread an end piece of sausage onto skewer followed by a piece of bacon, onion, bell pepper, and another piece of bacon. Repeat using center sausage pieces and finishing with end piece (center sausage pieces will be "sandwiched" between bacon). Repeat with remaining skewers and ingredients.

3. Place skewers on hot, oiled grill and cook 16 to 20 minutes, about 4 to 5 minutes per side. Brush with Barbecue Sauce with each turn.

4. Serve kabobs with additional Barbecue Sauce on the side (optional).

L.A. Cart Dogs

servings 4 **prep time** 15 minutes
grilling time 16 minutes

YOU WILL NEED
Oil
Wooden toothpicks

4	**hearty beef franks, *Ball Park*®**
4	**slices thick-cut bacon, *Oscar Mayer*®**
1	**white onion, sliced in rings**
1	**tablespoon extra-virgin olive oil, *Bertolli*®**
	Hot dog buns, toasted
	Sauerkraut, *Claussen*®
	Nacho sliced jalapeños, *Embasa*® (sliced pickled jalapeños)
	Sweet relish, *Vlasic*®
	Condiments (such as yellow mustard and ketchup)

INDOOR METHOD:
Preheat broiler. Prepare beef franks and onions as directed. Place franks and sliced onions on a wire rack over foil-lined sheet pan or broiler pan. Place 4 to 6 inches from heat source. Cook for 3 to 4 minutes per side or until bacon is crispy. (Watch onions closely so they don't burn.) Serve as directed.

1. Set up grill for direct cooking over medium heat (see page 19). Oil grate when ready to start cooking.

2. Wrap each frank in a slice of bacon, securing the ends with toothpicks; set aside. Toss onion slices with olive oil.

3. Place bacon-wrapped franks and onion slices on hot, oiled grill. Cook 16 to 20 minutes, about 4 to 5 minutes per side. Turn onions every time you turn franks. Remove franks and onions from grill. Remove toothpicks from franks.

4. Serve franks hot on toasted buns with grilled onions, sauerkraut, jalapeños, sweet relish, and condiments.

Pizzas and Quesadillas

Spread the word and the sauce—pizzas and quesadillas are great on the grill. It is, after all, how the Italians intended, smoking in flavor over a wood-burning fire. I could eat pizza every day, all day—and now you can too. Beef fajitas, chicken Caesar salad, barbecued shrimp—any entrée becomes pizza-perfect when ladled over a ready-made tortilla or a quick-mix crust. Topped with prosciutto and figs, it becomes upper-crust fare; pile on the sausage and eggs, and you've got comfort food. Any way you slice it, quesadillas and pizza round out a meal. Serve them whole or portion them out in bite-size nibbles to make a scrumptious starter or snack.

The Recipes

Southwest BBQ Chicken Pizza

servings 4 prep time 15 minutes
grilling time 10 minutes

YOU WILL NEED
Oil
Cookie sheet

1	**can (13.8-ounce) refrigerated pizza crust dough, *Pillsbury*®**
¹/₂	**cup mesquite grilling sauce, *McCormick*® *Grill Mates*®**
2	**cups shredded Monterey Jack cheese, *Kraft*®**
¹/₄	**cup thinly sliced red onion**
1	**cup frozen pepper stir-fry, thawed and drained, *Birds Eye*®**
1	**package (6-ounce) Southwest grilled chicken strips, *Louis Rich*®**
2	**tablespoons nacho sliced jalapeños, *Embasa*® (or pickled jalapeño slices)**
¹/₄	**cup crumbled cotija cheese**
2	**tablespoons chopped fresh cilantro**
	Fresh cilantro leaves (optional)

INDOOR METHOD:
Preheat oven to 425 degrees F. Lightly spray a cookie sheet with nonstick vegetable cooking spray. Carefully unroll pizza dough and place on prepared cookie sheet. Press out dough with fingers to form 13×9-inch rectangle. Bake about 7 minutes or just until crust begins to brown. Remove crust from oven and top as directed in step 3. Return to oven for 8 to 10 minutes or until crust is golden brown and cheese is bubbly and melted. Serve as directed.

1. Set up grill for direct cooking over medium heat (see page 19). Oil grate when ready to start cooking.

2. Carefully remove pizza dough from can. Unroll dough and place on hot, oiled grill. Cook 2 minutes. Using a cookie sheet, turn crust over.

3. Spread mesquite sauce over crust, leaving a 1-inch border. Top with Monterey Jack cheese, onion slices, pepper stir-fry, and chicken strips. Sprinkle with jalapeños, cotija cheese, and the chopped cilantro.

4. Cover grill. Cook for 8 to 10 minutes or until cheese is bubbly and melted. Using the cookie sheet, remove pizza from the grill.

5. Garnish pizza with additional fresh cilantro leaves (optional) and serve hot.

White Pizza

servings 4 **prep time** 15 minutes
grilling time 10 minutes

YOU WILL NEED
Oil
Cookie sheet

INDOOR METHOD:
Preheat oven to
425 degrees F. Lightly
spray cookie sheet with
nonstick vegetable
cooking spray; set aside.
Carefully unroll pizza
dough and place on
prepared cookie sheet.
Press out dough with
fingers to form
13×9-inch rectangle.
Bake about 7 minutes or
just until crust begins to
brown. Remove crust
from oven and top as
directed in step 3. Return
to oven for 8 to
10 minutes or until crust
is golden and cheese is
bubbly and melted.
Serve as directed.

1	**can (13.8-ounce) refrigerated pizza crust dough, *Pillsbury*®**
1/2	**cup roasted garlic Alfredo sauce, *Classico*®**
2	**cups shredded Italian 5-cheese blend, *Kraft*®**
1/4	**onion, thinly sliced**
1	**package (6-ounce) grilled chicken strips, *Louis Rich*®**
4	**roasted garlic cloves, *Christopher Ranch*®**
1/4	**cup shredded Parmesan cheese, *Kraft*®**
1	**teaspoon Italian seasoning, *McCormick*®**
	Fresh sprigs of rosemary (optional)

1. Set up grill for direct cooking over medium heat (see page 19). Oil grate when ready to start cooking.

2. Carefully remove pizza dough from can. Unroll dough and place on hot, oiled grill. Cook 2 minutes. Using a cookie sheet, turn crust over.

3. Spread Alfredo sauce over pizza, leaving a 1-inch border. Top with remaining ingredients (except the rosemary sprigs) in the order listed. Cover grill. Cook 8 to 10 minutes or until cheese is bubbly and melted. Using the cookie sheet, remove pizza from grill.

4. Garnish pizza with fresh rosemary sprigs (optional) and serve hot.

Chicken Caesar Salad Pizza

servings 4 **prep time** 20 minutes
grilling time 14 minutes

YOU WILL NEED
Oil
Large bowl
Cookie sheet

12   ounces chicken breast tenders
$^1/_2$ cup plus 2 tablespoons Caesar salad dressing, *Wish-Bone®*
1   12-inch thin pizza crust, *Boboli®*
1$^3/_4$ cups shredded mozzarella and Asiago cheese blend,
      Sargento® Bistro Blends®
$^1/_4$ cup shredded Parmesan cheese, *Kraft®*

FOR CAESAR SALAD TOPPING:
4   cups hearts of romaine, shredded, *Ready Pac®*
1   tablespoon lemon juice, *ReaLemon®*
$^1/_4$ cup Caesar salad dressing, *Wish-Bone®*
$^1/_4$ cup shredded Parmesan cheese, *Kraft®*
1   cup seasoned croutons, *Marie Callender's®*

1. Set up grill for direct cooking over medium heat (see page 19). Oil grate when ready to start cooking.

INDOOR METHOD:
Preheat oven to 450 degrees F. Prepare chicken as directed. In a large skillet, heat 2 tablespoons of vegetable oil. When oil is hot, add chicken tenders to the skillet. Cook for 4 to 6 minutes or until cooked through, turning once or twice. Remove from skillet and arrange on pizza. Bake for 8 to 10 minutes or until cheese is bubbly and melted. Serve as directed.

2. In a large bowl, toss chicken tenders with $^1/_2$ cup of the Caesar salad dressing; set aside. Brush pizza crust with remaining 2 tablespoons of Caesar dressing. Top with the cheese blend and the $^1/_4$ cup Parmesan cheese; set aside.

3. Remove chicken from marinade; discard marinade. Place chicken on hot, oiled grill. Cook for 3 to 4 minutes per side or until cooked through. Remove from grill and place on top of pizza crust.

4. Using a cookie sheet, transfer pizza to grill. Cover grill. Cook 8 to 10 minutes or until cheese is bubbly and melted.

5. Meanwhile, for the Caesar Salad Topping, toss shredded romaine with lemon juice. Add the $^1/_4$ cup Caesar salad dressing and the $^1/_4$ cup Parmesan cheese. Toss gently to coat.

6. Using the cookie sheet, remove pizza from grill. Cover pizza surface with the Caesar Salad Topping and garnish with croutons. Serve hot.

Meaty Stuffed Pizza

servings 4 **prep time** 30 minutes
cooking time 6 minutes **grilling time** 10 minutes

In Naples, they call it "pizza pie" and that's exactly what it is—a savory blend of meats, mushrooms, and olives combined with a marinara and mozzarella sauce and stuffed between two hand-rolled crusts. It's hot, hearty, and grill-baked to a doughy delight—the ultimate for pizza purists.

YOU WILL NEED
Oil
Large bowl
Plastic wrap
Large skillet
2 cookie sheets
Cornmeal

FOR PIZZA CRUST:
2   **packages (6.5 ounces each) pizza crust mix, *Betty Crocker*®**
2   **teaspoons Italian seasoning, *McCormick*®**
1   **cup hot water**

FOR FILLING:
8   **ounces lean ground beef**
8   **ounces hot Italian sausage, casings removed**
1   **jar (2.5-ounce) sliced mushrooms, drained, *Green Giant*®**
1   **can (2.25-ounce) sliced ripe olives, drained**
2   **cups shredded mozzarella cheese, *Kraft*®**
1   **cup marinara sauce, *Prego*®**

INDOOR METHOD:
Preheat oven to 425 degrees F. Lightly spray a cookie sheet with nonstick vegetable cooking spray; set aside. Prepare stuffed pizza as directed. Place on prepared cookie sheet. Bake for 20 to 25 minutes or until golden brown. Serve as directed.

1. Set up grill for direct cooking over medium heat (see page 19). Oil grate when ready to start cooking. In a large mixing bowl, combine pizza crust mixes, Italian seasoning, and hot water. Stir about 20 times until a ball forms. Split ball in half; cover each with plastic wrap.

2. In a large skillet, cook ground beef and sausage over medium-high heat, stirring frequently to break up clumps. Cook 6 to 8 minutes or until done. Remove from heat and drain. Stir in mushrooms and olives. Stir in mozzarella cheese and marinara sauce; set aside.

3. Sprinkle a cookie sheet with cornmeal. Unwrap dough. On a lightly floured surface, press dough balls out into two 12-inch circles about ¼ inch thick; pinch together any holes. Transfer one dough circle to the prepared cookie sheet. Spoon meat mixture into center of dough circle. Top with second dough circle and crimp edges together. Gently pat entire surface of pizza until flat across the top.

4. Using a cookie sheet, transfer pizza to hot, oiled grill. Cover grill. Cook 5 to 6 minutes. Turn pizza with 2 cookie sheets.* Cook 5 to 6 minutes more. Remove from grill with a cookie sheet; cut into wedges and serve hot.

*TIP: Use 2 cookie sheets to turn pizza over—one to slide under the pizza and one to put over the top before flipping.

Beef Fajita Pizza

servings 4 **prep time** 10 minutes
grilling time 13 minutes

Fajitas are just plain fun. Here that same sizzle comes from stir-fried steak seasoned with Tex-Mex spices, grilled with peppers and onions, spooned onto a pillowy crust, and served à la mode with sour cream and guacamole. Slice the pizza generously for a main course or cut into bite-size pieces to offer it nacho-style.

YOU WILL NEED
Oil
Medium bowl
Cookie sheet

1   **package (16-ounce) frozen pepper stir-fry, thawed and drained,** *Birds Eye*®
8   **ounces beef stir-fry strips**
2   **tablespoons extra-virgin olive oil,** *Bertolli*®
2   **tablespoons taco seasoning mix,** *Lawry's*®
1   **12-inch thin pizza crust,** *Boboli*®
1/2   **cup lime-garlic salsa,** *Pace*®
2   **cups shredded Mexican blend cheese,** *Kraft*®
    Sour cream
    Purchased refrigerated guacamole
    Additional salsa
    Fresh cilantro sprig (optional)

INDOOR METHOD:
Preheat oven to 450 degrees F. Lightly spray a cookie sheet with nonstick vegetable cooking spray. Prepare pepper and beef strips as directed. In a large skillet, heat 2 tablespoons of vegetable oil. When oil is hot, add beef and pepper strips; cook for 5 minutes. Remove from pan; set aside. Remove pizza crust from package and place on a cookie sheet. Spread crust with salsa; sprinkle with cheese. Top with beef and peppers. Bake for 8 to 10 minutes or until cheese is bubbly and melted. Serve as directed.

1. Set up grill for direct cooking over medium heat (see page 19). Oil grate when ready to start cooking.

2. In a medium bowl, combine pepper strips, beef strips, oil, and taco seasoning; set aside.

3. Remove pizza crust from package and place on a cookie sheet. Spread with salsa; top with cheese. Set aside.

4. Place beef and pepper strips on hot, oiled grill.* Cook about 5 minutes total, turning as needed. Remove from grill and place on top of pizza.

5. Using a cookie sheet, transfer pizza to grill. Cover grill. Cook for 8 to 10 minutes or until cheese is bubbly and melted. Remove pizza from grill using the cookie sheet.

6. Top pizza with sour cream, guacamole, and salsa. Garnish with a fresh cilantro sprig (optional) and serve hot.

*****TIP:** If you own a grill wok, use it to cook the pepper stir-fry on the grill. If you must put the peppers directly on the grill, be careful not to let the peppers (or beef strips) fall between the grate when grilling.

Jerk Shrimp Pizza with Mango BBQ Sauce

servings 4 prep time 20 minutes
marinating time 30 minutes
grilling time 11 minutes

YOU WILL NEED
Large zip-top bag
Oil
Blender
Plate
Cookie sheet

FOR SHRIMP TOPPING:
8   ounces medium shrimp, peeled and deveined
1   cup Caribbean jerk marinade, *Lawry's®*

FOR MANGO BBQ SAUCE:
1¹/₂ cups frozen mango chunks, thawed and drained, *Dole's®*
¹/₃ cup BBQ sauce, *KC Masterpiece®*
2   tablespoons dark rum, *Myers's®*

FOR PIZZA:
1   can (13.8-ounce) refrigerated pizza dough, *Pillsbury®*
2   cups shredded mozzarella cheese, *Kraft®*
¹/₄ cup thinly sliced red onion
¹/₃ cup roasted red bell peppers, cut into strips, *Mezzetta®*
2   tablespoons finely chopped fresh cilantro

INDOOR METHOD:
Preheat oven to 425 degrees F. Prepare shrimp as directed. Lightly spray cookie sheet with nonstick vegetable cooking spray; set aside. Remove shrimp from marinade; discard marinade. In a large skillet, heat 2 tablespoons of oil. When oil is hot, add shrimp to skillet. Cook for 2 minutes per side. Remove shrimp from skillet; set aside. Carefully unroll dough and place on prepared cookie sheet. Press out pizza dough with fingers to form 13×9-inch rectangle. Bake about 7 minutes or until crust just begins to brown. Remove crust from oven and top as directed in step 5. Return to oven for 8 to 10 minutes or until crust is golden and cheese is bubbly and melted. Serve as directed.

1. In a large zip-top bag, combine shrimp and jerk marinade. Squeeze air out of bag and seal. Gently massage bag to coat shrimp. Marinate in refrigerator for 30 minutes.

2. Set up grill for direct cooking over medium heat (see page 19). Oil grate when ready to start cooking.

3. For Mango BBQ Sauce, in a blender, combine thawed mango chunks, BBQ sauce, and rum. Blend until smooth; set aside.

4. Remove shrimp from marinade; discard marinade. Place shrimp on hot, oiled grill. Cook for 1 minute per side. (Shrimp will not be fully cooked.) Transfer to a plate; set aside.

5. Carefully remove pizza dough from can. Unroll dough and place on hot, oiled grill. Cook 1 minute. Using a cookie sheet, turn crust over. Spread ¹/₂ cup Mango BBQ Sauce over pizza, leaving a 1-inch border. Top with cheese, onion, red peppers, shrimp, and chopped cilantro. Cover grill. Cook 8 to 10 minutes or until cheese is bubbly and melted. Using the cookie sheet, remove pizza from grill. Serve hot.

Mexican Pizzas

servings 4 prep time 15 minutes
microwaving time 4 minutes grilling time 4 minutes

YOU WILL NEED
Oil
Small bowl
Microwave-safe bowl
Cookie sheet

FOR SAUCE:
$^1/_4$ **cup salsa, *Pace*®**
$^1/_4$ **cup sour cream**

FOR PIZZA:
4 **garlic-herb wraps, *Mission*® (or any 10-inch tortillas)**
2 **cups shredded Mexican cheese blend, *Kraft*®**
1 **can (16-ounce) refried black beans, *Rosarita*®**
1 **package (18-ounce) precooked ground beef for tacos, *Old El Paso*®**
$^1/_2$ **red onion, diced**
2 **cups shredded lettuce**
1 **tomato, diced**
    Nacho sliced jalapeños, *Embasa*® (or sliced pickled jalapeños)
    (optional)

INDOOR METHOD:
Preheat oven to
400 degrees F. Prepare
as directed in steps
2 through 4. In a
large skillet, heat
1 tablespoon vegetable
oil over medium heat.
When oil is hot, carefully
place one of the pizzas in
the skillet. Cook each
side of pizza for 1 to
2 minutes or until golden
brown, turning with a
large spatula. Transfer
pizza to a cookie sheet.
Repeat with remaining
pizza, adding oil as
needed. Spread pizzas
with warmed black
beans; top with taco
meat and onion. Bake
5 minutes. Remove from
oven; serve as directed.

1. Set up grill for direct cooking over medium heat (see page 19). Oil grate when ready to start cooking.

2. In a small bowl, combine salsa and sour cream; set aside.

3. Lay out 2 garlic-herb wraps; sprinkle with cheese blend. Top with remaining wraps; set aside.

4. In a microwave-safe bowl, cook refried black beans in microwave oven on high (100% power) for 4 to 6 minutes or until heated through, stirring twice.

5. Using a cookie sheet, place cheese-filled wraps on hot, oiled grill. Cook for 2 minutes; turn over. Divide refried beans between cheese-filled wraps. Spread evenly over the tops of the pizzas, leaving a $^1/_2$-inch border. Top beans with taco meat and onion. Cover grill; cook 2 minutes. Using the cookie sheet, remove pizza from grill.

6. Top with lettuce and tomato; drizzle with salsa-sour cream mixture. Garnish with sliced jalapeños (optional) and serve hot.

Breakfast Pizza

servings 4 **prep time** 20 minutes
grilling time 8 minutes

Breakfast meets dinner in an Italian spin on the morning meal—sausage and eggs scrambled with tomato and cheeses and served atop a ready-made pizza crust. It's an omelet with a new attitude: a make and munch meal-in-one that will have even the most resolute breakfast skipper rising, shining, and maybe even sharing.

YOU WILL NEED
Oil
Medium skillet
Cookie sheet

2	**tablespoons butter**
4	**eggs, lightly beaten**
2	**8-inch pizza crusts, *Boboli*® (or one 12-inch pizza crust)**
1	**tablespoon extra-virgin olive oil, *Bertolli*®**
1	**medium tomato, thinly sliced (reserve two tomato slices for the pizza tops; optional)**
2	**cups shredded Colby-Jack cheese blend, *Kraft*®**
4	**fully cooked sausage patties, crumbled, *Jimmy Dean*®**
¹/₄	**cup shredded Parmesan cheese, *Kraft*®**
1	**teaspoon Italian seasoning, *McCormick*®**

INDOOR METHOD:
Preheat oven to 450 degrees F. Lightly spray a cookie sheet or pizza pan with nonstick vegetable cooking spray. Prepare pizza as directed. Place on prepared pan. Bake for 8 to 10 minutes or until cheese is bubbly and melted. Remove from oven. Serve as directed.

1. Set up grill for direct cooking over medium heat (see page 19). Oil grate when ready to start cooking.

2. In a medium skillet, melt butter over medium heat. Add eggs and scramble; set aside.

3. Lay out pizza crusts and brush each with oil. Layer with tomato slices, cheese blend, crumbled sausage, and scrambled eggs. Top with reserved tomato slices (optional). Sprinkle with Parmesan cheese and Italian seasoning.

4. Using a cookie sheet, slide pizzas onto hot, oiled grill. Cover grill. Cook 8 to 10 minutes or until cheese is bubbly and melted. Using the cookie sheet, remove pizzas from grill. Serve hot.

Smoked Turkey, Brie, and Apricot Quesadillas

servings 4 **prep time** 20 minutes
grilling time 6 minutes

YOU WILL NEED
Oil
Small bowl
Large spatula or cookie sheet

8	taco-size flour tortillas, *Mission®*
5	ounces Brie cheese, sliced
8	ounces smoked turkey breast, thinly sliced
1/2	cup apricot spreadable fruit, *Smucker's®*
1/2	cup shredded Monterey Jack cheese, *Kraft®*
2	cups fresh mixed herbs (such as parsley, basil, tarragon, chives, mint, and/or oregano)
1	tablespoon fresh lemon juice
	Salt and ground black pepper

INDOOR METHOD:
Prepare quesadillas as directed. In a large skillet, heat 1 tablespoon vegetable oil over medium heat. When oil is hot, add 1 to 2 quesadillas (quesadillas must lie flat; don't overcrowd). Cook both sides of quesadillas for 2 to 3 minutes or until golden brown, turning with a large spatula. Continue with remaining quesadillas, adding more oil as needed. Serve as directed.

1. Set up grill for direct cooking over medium heat (see page 19). Oil grate when ready to cook.

2. Lay out 4 tortillas. Top each tortilla with one-fourth of the Brie cheese, smoked turkey, apricot spreadable fruit, and Jack cheese. Top with remaining tortillas.

3. In a small bowl, toss to combine herbs and lemon juice. Season with salt and pepper; set aside.

4. Using a large spatula, carefully place quesadillas on hot, oiled grill. Cook for 3 to 4 minutes per side or until cheese is bubbly and melted. Remove from grill.

5. Serve hot with mixed herbs on the side.

Shrimp Club
Quesadillas

servings 4 **prep time** 15 minutes
grilling time 12 minutes

YOU WILL NEED
Oil
2 cookie sheets
Medium bowl

6	taco-size flour tortillas, *Mission*®
1	cup shredded Monterey Jack cheese, *Kraft*®
8	ounces medium cooked shrimp, tails and shells removed
1	avocado, pitted and sliced
½	cup real bacon bits, *Hormel*®

INDOOR METHOD:
Preheat oven to 400 degrees F. In a large skillet, heat 1 tablespoon vegetable oil over medium heat. When oil is hot, carefully place 1 to 2 tortillas in skillet (tortillas must lie flat; don't overcrowd). Cook for 1 to 2 minutes per side or just until golden brown. Transfer fried tortillas to a paper towel-lined cookie sheet. Repeat with the remaining 5 tortillas. Assemble as directed in step 3 (using all fried tortillas). Place on cookie sheet (discard paper towels). Bake for 8 to 10 minutes or until cheese is melted. Serve as directed.

1. Set up grill for direct cooking over medium heat (see page 19). Oil grate when ready to start cooking.

2. Prepare all the ingredients and have them ready at the grill. Place 2 tortillas on hot, oiled grill. (These will be center tortillas of quesadilla.) Cook 1 to 2 minutes per side or until crisp. Remove; set aside.

3. Lay out 2 uncooked tortillas. Sprinkle each with ¼ cup of cheese. Divide shrimp among the 2 tortillas; distribute evenly over top. Place grilled tortillas on top of shrimp-topped tortillas. Top grilled tortillas with remaining cheese, sliced avocado, and bacon bits. Set the 2 remaining tortillas on top.

4. Using a cookie sheet, carefully slide quesadillas onto hot, oiled grill. Cook 5 to 6 minutes per side* or until cheese is bubbly and melted.

5. Remove quesadillas from grill. Cut into wedges; serve hot.

*****TIP:** Use 2 cookie sheets to turn quesadilla over—one to slide under the quesadilla and one to put over the top before flipping.

Smoked Salmon Quesadillas

servings 4 **prep time** 10 minutes
grilling time 6 minutes

YOU WILL NEED
Oil
Small bowl
Large spatula or cookie sheet

8	taco-size flour tortillas, *Mission*®
5	ounces Boursin cheese, softened
4	ounces smoked salmon, *Echo Falls*®
1/2	cup shredded Monterey Jack cheese, *Kraft*®
1	tablespoon capers, *Star*®
1/2	cup sour cream
1	tablespoon fresh dill, finely chopped
1	avocado, sliced
1 1/2	cups halved cherry tomatoes, *Nature Sweet*®
1/2	red onion, cut into very thin wedges
	Fresh dill sprigs (optional)

INDOOR METHOD:
Prepare quesadillas as directed. In a large skillet, heat 1 tablespoon vegetable oil over medium heat. When oil is hot, carefully place 1 to 2 quesadillas in skillet (quesadillas must lie flat; don't overcrowd). Cook both sides of quesadillas for 2 to 3 minutes or until golden brown; turning with a large spatula. Repeat with remaining quesadillas. Serve as directed.

1. Set up grill for direct cooking over medium heat (see page 19). Oil grate when ready to start cooking.

2. Lay out 4 tortillas; spread each with one-fourth of the Boursin cheese. Divide salmon, Jack cheese, and capers evenly and place on top of Boursin on each tortilla. Top with remaining tortillas.

3. In a small bowl, combine sour cream and dill; set aside.

4. Using a large spatula, place quesadillas on hot, oiled grill. Cook 3 to 4 minutes per side or until cheese is melted and bubbly. Remove from grill with spatula.

5. Top with sliced avocado, halved cherry tomatoes, onion, and sour cream-dill mixture. Garnish with fresh dill sprigs (optional). Serve hot.

Prosciutto, Fig, and Goat Cheese Quesadillas

servings 4 **prep time** 10 minutes
grilling time 6 minutes

The rustic flirts with the refined in this trendy trattoria-style quesadilla that blends the earthy charm of Provence, France, with the sunny delicacies of northern Italy. Spicy prosciutto resides companionably with nutty fig and creamy goat cheese atop a tortilla in a new old-world classic. Serve it solo as an entrée or as a starter for a traditional meal.

YOU WILL NEED
Oil
Large spatula or cookie sheet

8	taco-size flour tortillas, *Mission*®
5	ounces creamy goat cheese, *Silver Goat*®
3	ounces thinly sliced prosciutto
4	fresh figs, sliced
¹/₂	cup shredded Monterey Jack cheese, *Kraft*®
¹/₂	cup fig preserves,* *Braswell's*®

INDOOR METHOD:
Prepare quesadillas as directed. In a large skillet, heat 1 tablespoons vegetable oil over medium heat. When oil is hot, carefully place 1 to 2 quesadillas in skillet (quesadillas must lie flat; don't overcrowd). Cook both sides for 2 to 3 minutes or until golden brown, turning with a large spatula. Repeat with remaining quesadillas. adding oil as necessary. Serve as directed.

1. Set up grill for direct cooking over medium heat (see page 19). Oil grate when ready to start cooking.

2. Lay out 4 tortillas; spread each with one-fourth of the goat cheese. Divide prosciutto and figs evenly and place on top of goat cheese. Top with Jack cheese and remaining tortillas.

3. Using a large spatula, place quesadillas on hot, oiled grill. Cook 3 to 4 minutes per side or until cheese is bubbly and melted. Remove from grill with spatula.

4. Serve hot with fig preserves on the side.

*NOTE: If fresh figs are not available or in season, use 2 tablespoons fig preserves in place of the 4 fresh figs.

Sides

In this hectic life, it's hard enough to get the main dish on the table, much less anything else. This chapter is full of fresh-from-the-pantry ideas created from off-the-shelf staples that I pull out in a pinch and reinvent to make creative combos. Grilled Caesar salad is a great preamble to a sizzling steak, jalapeño pepper poppers spice up a backyard burger, and garlicky mesquite toast goes sidesaddle with shrimp on the barbie—or swap them around to give old favorites new life. Every single side makes a delightful dinner companion to every single entrée, giving you hundreds of options to pique any palate. Or serve several sides together for a vegetarian smorgasbord. Go ahead—choose sides. Then add a drink and dessert for a full-course meal.

The Recipes

Sweet and Spicy Chili

servings 4 **prep time** 10 minutes
cooking time 30 minutes

YOU WILL NEED
Large skillet

1	**pound lean ground beef**
2	**cans (15 ounces each) vegetarian chili with beans, *Hormel*®**
1	**can (10-ounce) diced tomatoes with green chiles, *Ro-Tel*®**
¹⁄₄	**cup honey, *Sue Bee*®**
¹⁄₂	**teaspoon pumpkin pie spice, *McCormick*®**
	Shredded cheese
	Chopped red onion
	Tortilla chips (optional)

1. In a large skillet, cook ground beef over medium-high heat. Add vegetarian chili, diced tomatoes, honey, and pumpkin pie spice; bring to a boil. Reduce heat and simmer for 25 to 30 minutes, stirring occasionally, until thickened.

2. Top with shredded cheese and chopped red onion. Serve hot with tortilla chips (optional) on the side.

Hoppin' John Salad

servings 8 **prep time** 10 minutes
cooking time 25 minutes **standing time** 5 minutes

The famous pea pilaf migrated to U.S. rice plantations from Africa. Southern cooks put their stamp on it with field peas and dirty rice and called it Hoppin' John. This spicy version adds chunky salsa and red onion.

YOU WILL NEED
Medium saucepan
Sheet pan
Large bowl

2¹⁄₂	**cups low-sodium chicken broth, *Swanson*®**
2	**tablespoons canola oil, *Wesson*®**
1	**box (8-ounce) dirty rice mix, *Zatarain's*®**
1	**can (15-ounce) black-eyed peas, drained**
1	**cup chunky salsa, *Pace*®**
2	**stalks celery, diced**
1	**carrot, diced**
¹⁄₂	**red onion, diced**
	Fresh flat-leaf parsley sprig (optional)

1. In a medium saucepan, bring chicken broth and oil to a boil over high heat. Add dirty rice mix; return to boil. Reduce heat; cover and simmer for 25 minutes.

2. Remove rice from heat; let stand 5 minutes. Spread on a sheet pan; let cool to room temperature. Transfer rice to large bowl. Add remaining ingredients; toss to combine. Garnish with flat-leaf parsley sprig (optional).

Borracho Beans

servings 4 **prep time** 15 minutes
cooking time 25 minutes

South of the border, they call them "drunk" beans because a bottle of beer is used as the broth. When brewed with pinto beans, bacon, and tomatoes and green chiles, it all becomes a peppery puree—cooled with a chaser of cilantro and fresh lime. Serve with tortillas for dipping, if desired.

YOU WILL NEED
Medium saucepan

2	cans (16 ounces each) pinto beans, *Bush's®*
1	can (10-ounce) diced tomatoes and green chiles, *Ro-Tel®*
1	can (4-ounce) diced green chiles, *La Victoria®*
¹/₂	cup frozen diced onions, *C&W®*
1	teaspoon crushed garlic, *Christopher Ranch®*
1	bottle (12-ounce) Mexican beer, *Negro Modelo®*
¹/₃	cup real bacon pieces, *Hormel®*
¹/₄	cup finely chopped fresh cilantro
1	lime, sliced into wedges

1. In a medium saucepan over medium-high heat, stir to combine all ingredients (except cilantro and lime wedges). Bring to boil; reduce heat to medium-low heat and simmer for 20 minutes.

2. Stir in cilantro and serve with lime wedges.

Mesquite BBQ Beans

servings 4 **prep time** 10 minutes
grilling time 30 minutes

YOU WILL NEED
Medium bowl
8-inch cast-iron skillet

1	can (28-ounce) baked beans, *Bush's®*
¹/₄	cup mesquite grilling sauce, *McCormick® Grill Mates®*
¹/₄	cup real bacon pieces, *Hormel®*
2	tablespoons spicy brown mustard, *Gulden's®*
5	slices center-cut bacon, *Oscar Mayer®*

1. Set up grill for direct cooking over medium heat (see page 19).

2. In a medium bowl, stir to combine beans, mesquite sauce, bacon pieces, and mustard. Pour bean mixture into an 8-inch cast-iron skillet. Place bacon slices on top of the beans.

3. Place skillet on grill. Cover grill and cook for 30 minutes. Serve hot.

INDOOR METHOD:
Preheat oven to 350 degrees F. Prepare beans as directed. Pour into a 2-quart ovenproof casserole dish; top with bacon slices. Bake for 35 to 40 minutes or until thickened and bubbling. Serve as directed.

Bacon-Wrapped Cheese Corn

servings 4 **prep time** 20 minutes
grilling time 25 minutes

As if butter-drenched corn on the cob wasn't irresistible enough, wrap a strip of bacon around it, drizzle it with cheese, and watch its popularity soar. Roasted ears of cheese corn are a common street snack in Mexico. A four-cheese and mayonnaise sauce makes it picnic-perfect.

YOU WILL NEED
Small bowl
Aluminum foil

1	packet (1.5-ounce) four-cheese sauce mix, *Knorr*®
3	tablespoons mayonnaise, *Best Foods*® or *Hellmann's*®
4	ears corn, shucked and cleaned
4	slices thick-cut bacon, *Oscar Mayer*®

INDOOR METHOD:
Preheat oven to 425 degrees F. Prepare corn, wrapped in foil, as directed. Roast for 20 to 25 minutes. Serve hot.

1. Set up grill for direct cooking over medium heat (see page 19).

2. In a small bowl, sprinkle cheese sauce mix over mayonnaise; stir thoroughly. Brush corn with mixture. Wrap each ear with a bacon slice; wrap in foil.

3. Place on hot grill. Cook for 25 to 30 minutes or until corn is tender and bacon is cooked, turning often. Serve hot.

Grilled Texas Mesquite Toast

servings 8 **prep time** 5 minutes
microwaving time 1 minute
grilling time 1½ minutes

YOU WILL NEED
Microwave-safe bowl

4	tablespoons butter
3	tablespoons garlic spread, *Lawry's*®
½	teaspoon mesquite seasoning, *McCormick*® *Grill Mates*®
8	slices thick-slice white bread

1. Set up grill for direct cooking over medium heat (see page 19).

2. In a microwave-safe bowl, combine butter, garlic spread, and mesquite seasoning. Cook in microwave oven on high setting (100% power) about 1 minute.

3. Brush each slice of bread on one side with butter mixture.

4. Place bread, buttered sides down, on grill. Cook for 1 minute. (To obtain diagonal grill marks on bread, turn each slice one-quarter turn and grill for an additional 30 seconds.) Remove from grill and serve warm.

INDOOR METHOD:
Prepare bread as directed. Heat a skillet over medium heat. Place bread, buttered sides down, in skillet and cook about 2 minutes or until golden. Serve as directed.

Jalapeño Potato Salad

servings 6 prep time 5 minutes
chilling time 1 hour

YOU WILL NEED
Large bowl
Plastic wrap

2   **pounds deli potato salad**
2   **tablespoons diced jalapeños, *La Victoria*®**
1   **scallion (green onion), chopped**
1   **tablespoon finely chopped fresh cilantro**
1   **teaspoon Mexican seasoning, *McCormick*®**
6   **dashes chipotle pepper sauce, *Tabasco*®**
     Whole jalapeño peppers (optional)

1. In a large bowl, stir to combine all ingredients, except whole jalapeño peppers. Cover with plastic wrap and refrigerate 1 hour to allow flavors to blend.

2. Garnish with whole jalapeño peppers (optional). Serve chilled.

Texas Mashed Potato Salad

servings 6 prep time 10 minutes
microwaving time 18 minutes chilling time 2 hours

YOU WILL NEED
Microwave-safe bowl
Large bowl
Potato masher

1   **bag (28-ounce) frozen potatoes O'Brien, *Ore-Ida*®**
1   **tablespoon water**
2   **hard-cooked eggs, chopped**
¹/₂ **cup mayonnaise, *Best Foods*® or *Hellmann's*®**
¹/₄ **cup yellow mustard, *French's*®**
2   **tablespoons sweet pickle relish, *Vlasic*®**
     Salt and ground black pepper
     Paprika (optional)
     Fresh parsley leaves (optional)

1. Place potatoes in microwave-safe bowl with the water. Cover and cook in microwave oven on high setting (100% power) for 8 minutes. Stir; cover and cook 10 to 12 minutes more or until potatoes are tender. Drain. Transfer to a large bowl and refrigerate about 2 hours or until thoroughly chilled.

2. Remove potatoes from the refrigerator. Add eggs, mayonnaise, mustard, and relish. Mash with a potato masher until combined and potatoes are in small pieces. Season with salt and pepper to taste. Sprinkle with paprika and garnish with parsley (optional).

Waldorf Slaw

servings 4 prep time 10 minutes
chilling time 1 hour

YOU WILL NEED
Large bowl
Small bowl
Plastic wrap

1   bag (16-ounce) 3-color slaw mix, *Fresh Express®*
2   large Granny Smith apples, cored and diced small
1   cup chopped walnuts, *Blue Diamond®*
1/2   cup mayonnaise, *Best Foods®* or *Hellmann's®*
1/3   cup poppy seed dressing, *Knott's®*

1. In a large bowl, combine slaw mix, diced apples, and chopped walnuts; set aside.

2. In small bowl, stir to combine mayonnaise and poppy seed dressing. Pour dressing over slaw mixture and toss to combine.

3. Cover with plastic wrap and refrigerate 1 hour before serving.

Grilled Caesar Ranch Salad

servings 6 prep time 5 minutes
grilling time 1 minute

YOU WILL NEED
Oil
Small bowl

FOR DRESSING:
1   cup ranch dressing, *Hidden Valley®*
1/4   cup shredded Parmesan cheese, *Kraft®*
2   tablespoons fresh lemon juice
2   teaspoons Dijon mustard, *Grey Poupon®*
1/2   teaspoon crushed garlic, *Christopher Ranch®*
   Salt and ground black pepper

FOR SALAD:
1   package (3-ounce) romaine hearts, *Earthbound Farm®*
2   tablespoons extra-virgin olive oil, *Bertolli®*
   Salt and ground black pepper
   Caesar salad croutons, *Pepperidge Farm®*
   Additional Parmesan cheese

1. Set up grill for direct cooking over medium heat (see page 19). Oil grate when ready to start cooking.

2. In a small bowl, combine ranch dressing, the 1/4 cup Parmesan cheese, the lemon juice, mustard, and garlic. Season with salt and pepper; set aside.

3. Cut romaine hearts lengthwise, keeping core intact. Drizzle cut sides with olive oil and season with salt and pepper. Place romaine hearts, cut sides down, on hot, oiled grill. Grill 1 to 2 minutes or until grill marks form and romaine lettuce just begins to wilt.

4. Transfer to plates; drizzle with dressing. Garnish with croutons and additional Parmesan cheese.

Grilled Jalapeño Poppers

servings 4 prep time 20 minutes
grilling time 6 minutes

YOU WILL NEED
Oil
Wooden toothpicks

12 **large jalapeño peppers***
1 **cup Mexican blend shredded cheese, *Kraft*®**
6 **slices thick-cut bacon, *Oscar Mayer*®**

1. Set up grill for direct cooking over medium-high heat (see page 19). Oil grate when ready to start cooking.

INDOOR METHOD: Preheat oven to 400 degrees F. Prepare peppers as directed. Place on foil-lined sheet pan. Bake for 25 minutes or until bacon is cooked thoroughly and starting to crisp. Serve as directed.

2. Slice peppers from stem to tip on one side.* Carefully squeeze ends of peppers (like a change purse) and scoop out seeds and veins. Stuff peppers with cheese. Cut each bacon slice in half crosswise. Wrap each pepper with a piece of bacon and secure with a toothpick.

3. Place peppers on hot, oiled grill. Cook for 3 to 5 minutes per side or until bacon is cooked but not crisp. Remove toothpicks and serve hot.

*NOTE: Jalapeños can be very hot. Use caution and wear rubber gloves if you have skin sensitivity. Keep hands away from face and eyes. Wash hands thoroughly with warm water and soap when finished handling peppers.

Grilled Chili Fries

servings 4 prep time 5 minutes
grilling time 6 minutes

More fire, less fat. These five-alarm fries are guiltless on the grill. Swapping zippy chili seasoning for the more caloric chili makes them a health-smart choice. Forget ketchup—dip them in BBQ sauce or Dijon mustard.

YOU WILL NEED
Oil
Sheet pan

1 **bag (28-ounce) frozen steak fries, thawed, *Ore-Ida*®**
2 **tablespoons canola oil, *Wesson*®**
1 **tablespoon chili seasoning, *McCormick*®**
Purchased BBQ sauce
Dijon mustard

1. Set up grill for direct cooking over medium heat (see page 19). Oil grate when ready to start cooking.

2. On a sheet pan, drizzle fries with oil and sprinkle with chili seasoning. Toss to coat. Place fries on hot, oiled grill and cook for 3 to 5 minutes per side. Serve hot with BBQ sauce or Dijon mustard for dipping.

INDOOR METHOD: Preheat broiler. Place frozen fries on foil-lined sheet pan. Toss to coat with oil and chili seasoning. Broil fries for 8 to 12 minutes or until crispy, turning once. Serve as directed.

Desserts

Dessert is an exclamation point on a meal, a reminder that although beginnings are delicious with possibility, endings can be sweet as well. Dessert on the grill feels luxuriously indulgent, an unexpected reward to savor yourself or share with others. When I was younger, I thought joy was a toasted marshmallow. Then I added graham crackers and a Hershey® bar and discovered the ecstasy of s'mores. As a grown-up, I know that there are many layers of decadence—French toast grilled in Grand Marnier® and smothered with strawberries, gingery ice cream sandwiched between warm sugar cookies, peaches laced with tarragon and crowned with mounds of mascarpone cream. They're all so easy to make that anyone could do it. Just keep the grill going and dessert is served.

The Recipes

Triple Lemon Tartlets

servings 8 prep time 10 minutes
grilling time 14 minutes
cooking time 15 minutes

YOU WILL NEED
Medium saucepan
Eight 4¹/₂-inch tartlet pans
Foil baking pan

1   box (15-ounce) rolled refrigerated unbaked piecrusts, *Pillsbury®*
1   box (4.3-ounce) cook-and-serve lemon pudding mix, *Jell-O®*
4   egg yolks, slightly beaten
¹/₄ cup sugar
3   cups lemonade, *Minute Maid®*
2   teaspoons finely grated lemon zest
     Fresh raspberries and thin strips of lemon peel (optional)

INDOOR METHOD:
Preheat oven to 450 degrees F. Prepare tartlet shells as directed. Place tartlet shells on a sheet pan; bake for 10 to 12 minutes or until golden brown. Prepare lemon filling as directed. Evenly pour filling into tartlet shells. Cool in the refrigerator until set. Serve as directed.

1. Set up grill for indirect cooking over medium heat (no heat source under tartlets; see page 19). Unroll piecrusts. Lay tartlet pans upside down on unrolled crusts; cut piecrust into circles around the pans, leaving a 1-inch border. Press cutouts into pans. (Using 4¹/₂-inch tartlet pans, 2 tart shells can be cut from one crust. Gather scraps and reroll; cut out two more. Repeat with other crust.) Place tartlet shells on a foil baking pan and bake on hot grill for 14 to 18 minutes or until crusts are golden brown.

2. In a medium saucepan, whisk together pudding mix, egg yolks, sugar, and ¹/₂ cup of the lemonade until pudding mix dissolves. Stir in remaining lemonade and lemon zest. Bring mixture to a boil over medium heat; cook about 10 minutes, stirring constantly. Cool for 5 minutes, stirring occasionally. Evenly pour filling into shells. Cool in the refrigerator until set. Garnish with raspberries and lemon peel strips (optional).

Peaches with Mascarpone Cream

servings 6
prep time 15 minutes

YOU WILL NEED
2 medium bowls
Parfait or large martini glasses

1   bag (16-ounce) frozen peach slices, thawed
1   tablespoon fresh tarragon leaves
¹/₄ cup orange-flavor liqueur, *Grand Marnier®*
8   ounces mascarpone cheese
¹/₄ cup sugar
1   container (8-ounce) whipped topping, thawed, *Cool Whip®*
     Extra Creamy
¹/₂ cup crushed almond biscotti cookies
2   tablespoons sliced almonds, toasted

1. In a medium bowl, combine thawed peaches, tarragon, and orange-flavor liqueur. In another medium bowl, whisk mascarpone cheese and sugar until creamy. Whisk in thawed whipped topping.

2. Divide half of the mascarpone mixture among six parfait glasses. Top with peach mixture. Sprinkle with crushed biscotti and top with remaining mascarpone mixture. Sprinkle with toasted sliced almonds.

Upside-Down Apple Skillet Pie

servings 8 prep time 20 minutes
grilling time 20 minutes
cooling time 1 hour

YOU WILL NEED
10-inch cast-iron skillet or other ovenproof skillet
Wooden spoon
Dessert bowls

$^1/_2$	**cup butter (1 stick)**
$^1/_2$	**cup packed brown sugar**
1	**teaspoon cinnamon**
1	**can (21-ounce) apple pie filling, *Comstock®***
2	**cups pre-sliced apples, *Ready Pac®***
1	**rolled refrigerated unbaked piecrust, *Pillsbury®* ($^1/_2$ of a 15-ounce box)**
2	**tablespoons frozen apple juice concentrate, thawed, *Minute Maid®***
1	**tablespoon granulated sugar**
	Vanilla ice cream (optional)

INDOOR METHOD:
Preheat oven to 425 degrees F. Follow step 2, except cook mixture over medium-high heat in a 10-inch cast-iron or ovenproof skillet. Once mixture begins to bubble, follow step 3. Bake for 30 to 35 minutes or until crust is golden brown. Remove from oven and let cool at least 1 hour. Serve as directed.

1. Set up grill for direct cooking over medium-high heat (see page 19).

2. For filling, place a 10-inch cast-iron skillet on the grill. Add butter. When butter has melted, stir in brown sugar and cinnamon. Cook until mixture begins to bubble. Stir in apple pie filling and apple slices.

3. Unroll piecrust and place over skillet. With a wooden spoon, push edge of piecrust into skillet, making sure to seal the skillet all around the edge. Brush crust with apple juice concentrate and sprinkle with granulated sugar. Cut slit in top of crust to allow steam to escape.

4. Cover grill and bake for 20 to 30 minutes or until crust is golden brown. Remove from grill. Cool at least 1 hour.

5. Cut pie into wedges. Scoop each serving into a dessert bowl. Top with vanilla ice cream (optional).

Strawberry Skillet Shortcake

servings 8 **prep time** 20 minutes
standing time 1 hour **grilling time** 15 minutes

YOU WILL NEED
Medium bowl
Small bowl
10-inch cast-iron skillet or other ovenproof skillet

1	**pound frozen unsweetened strawberries, quartered and thawed**
³/₄	**cup sugar**
1	**teaspoon cinnamon, *McCormick*®**
1	**can (16.3-ounce) *Pillsbury*® *Grands!*® *Southern style biscuits***
2	**tablespoons butter**
	Fresh strawberries, sliced (optional)
	Whipped topping, *Cool Whip*® (optional)

INDOOR METHOD:
Prepare frozen strawberries as directed. Preheat oven to 350 degrees F. Coat a 2½- to 3-quart baking dish with butter; set aside. Follow step 3 as directed. Spoon strawberries into prepared baking dish and top with cinnamon-sugar biscuits. Bake for 20 to 25 minutes or until mixture is bubbling. Remove from the oven; cool slightly. Serve as directed.

1. In a medium bowl, combine thawed strawberries and ½ cup of the sugar. Let stand for 1 hour to allow flavors to blend, stirring occasionally.

2. Set up grill for direct cooking over medium-high heat (see page 19).

3. In a small bowl, combine the remaining ¼ cup sugar and the cinnamon. Remove biscuits from the can and separate into biscuits. Roll each biscuit in the cinnamon-sugar mixture.

4. Coat a cast-iron skillet with butter. Add strawberry-sugar mixture. Arrange biscuits over strawberries. Place skillet on grill. Cover grill and bake for 15 to 20 minutes or until bubbly. Remove from grill; cool slightly. Serve with sliced fresh strawberries and whipped topping (optional).

Kahlúa® S'more Pie

servings 8 **prep time** 15 minutes
grilling time 45 minutes

A childhood classic is reinvented for grown-ups. Velvety chocolate and gooey marshmallows are spiked with Kahlúa® and scooped into a golden graham cracker crust that makes the years melt away. Being grown-up is better after all.

YOU WILL NEED
Large bowl
Foil sheet pan

4	**eggs**
1^1/$_2$	**cups sugar**
1	**can (5-ounce) evaporated milk, *Carnation*®**
^{1}/$_2$	**stick butter, melted**
^{1}/$_4$	**cup *Kahlúa*® (coffee-flavor liqueur)**
3	**tablespoons unsweetened cocoa powder, *Hershey's*®**
1	**premade graham cracker piecrust (6-ounce), *Keebler*® *Ready Crust*®**
2	**cups miniature marshmallows, *Kraft*®**

INDOOR METHOD:
Preheat oven to 350 degrees F. Prepare pie filling as directed. Place piecrust on sheet pan and fill with chocolate mixture. Bake for 50 to 55 minutes. About 5 to 10 minutes before pie is finished, mound marshmallows in the center of the pie (they will spread as they melt). Continue baking until marshmallows are golden and melted. Serve as directed.

1. Set up grill for indirect cooking over medium heat (no heat source under pie; page 19).

2. In a large bowl, whisk together eggs and sugar until thoroughly combined and pale yellow. Whisk in evaporated milk, melted butter, Kahlúa®, and cocoa powder; set aside.

3. Place piecrust on foil sheet pan on the grill away from heat source. Fill piecrust with chocolate mixture. Cover grill and bake for 40 to 50 minutes or just until pie is set and a knife inserted in the center comes out with a small bit of filling on it.

4. Mound miniature marshmallows in center of pie (they will spread as they melt). Cover grill and bake 5 to 10 minutes or until marshmallows are golden brown and melted.

5. Remove from grill and let cool slightly. Serve warm.

Skillet Cherry Cobbler

servings 8 **prep time** 20 minutes
grilling time 20 minutes
cooling time 1 hour

YOU WILL NEED
Large bowl
10-inch cast-iron skillet or other ovenproof skillet

INDOOR METHOD:
Preheat oven to
350 degrees F. Prepare
baking mix batter as
directed; set aside.
Follow directions for
preparing cherry
mixture, except cook
mixture in a saucepan
over medium-high heat
until it begins to bubble.
Transfer to 2-quart
baking dish. Pour baking
mix batter over top of
cherry mixture. Place
cobbler in oven. Bake for
35 to 40 minutes or until
golden brown and
toothpick inserted into
the top crust comes out
clean. Remove from
oven; cool 1 hour. Serve
as directed.

1$\frac{1}{2}$ **cups baking mix, *Bisquick*®**
$\frac{3}{4}$ **cup sugar**
$\frac{3}{4}$ **cup evaporated milk, *Carnation*®**
1   **teaspoon almond extract**
$\frac{1}{2}$ **cup butter (1 stick)**
$\frac{3}{4}$ **cup sugar**
1   **can (21-ounce) cherry pie filling, *Comstock*® *More Fruit*®**
1   **cup frozen cherries, thawed, *Dole*®**
     Whipped topping, *Cool Whip*® or vanilla ice cream (optional)

1. Set up grill for direct cooking over medium heat (see page 19).

2. In a large bowl, combine baking mix, $\frac{3}{4}$ cup sugar, evaporated milk, and almond extract. Whisk until smooth. Set aside.

3. Place 10-inch cast-iron skillet on the hot grill and add butter. When the butter has melted, stir in $\frac{3}{4}$ cup sugar. When sugar mixture begins to bubble, stir in pie filling and thawed frozen cherries. Pour baking mix batter over top. Cover grill and bake for 20 to 30 minutes or until golden brown and toothpick inserted into the top crust comes out clean.

4. Remove from grill. Cool 1 hour. Serve cobbler warm with whipped topping or scoops of vanilla ice cream (optional).

Grand Marnier® French Toast with Strawberries

servings 6 **prep time** 20 minutes
standing time 1 hour **grilling time** 6 minutes

YOU WILL NEED
Oil
Large bowl
Shallow bowl

1	**pound frozen unsweetened strawberries, quartered and thawed**
¼	**cup sugar**
2	**tablespoons *Grand Marnier*® (orange-flavor liqueur)**
3	**eggs**
½	**cup milk**
¼	**cup *Grand Marnier*® (orange-flavor liqueur)**
2	**tablespoons sugar**
6	**slices thick-sliced bread, cut in half diagonally**
	Whipped topping, *Cool Whip*®

1. In a large bowl, combine strawberries, the ¼ cup sugar, and the 2 tablespoons Grand Marnier®. Let stand 1 hour to allow flavors to blend, stirring occasionally.

2. Set up grill for direct cooking over medium heat (see page 19). Oil grate when ready to start cooking.

3. In a shallow bowl, whisk together eggs, milk, the ¼ cup Grand Marnier®, and the 2 tablespoons sugar. Coat each piece of bread on both sides with egg mixture. Place coated pieces on hot, oiled grill. Cook 3 to 4 minutes per side.

4. To serve, place one piece of French toast on a plate. Top with berries and whipped topping. Add another piece of toast and repeat layers. Repeat with remaining ingredients. Serve immediately.

INDOOR METHOD:
Prepare bread pieces as directed. On a griddle, melt 2 to 3 tablespoons of butter over medium-high heat. Cook prepared bread pieces about 3 minutes per side or until golden brown. Serve as directed.

Red Velvet Bars

servings 8 **prep time** 20 minutes
grilling time 40 minutes

YOU WILL NEED
Two 13×9-inch foil baking pans
Nonstick cooking spray
Large mixing bowl
Electric mixer
Medium mixing bowl

FOR CAKE LAYER:
1   **box (18.25-ounce) German chocolate cake mix, *Betty Crocker*®**
1/2   **cup butter (1 stick), softened**
1   **egg**
1   **ounce red food coloring, *McCormick*®**

FOR CREAM CHEESE LAYER:
16   **ounces cream cheese, softened, *Philadelphia*®**
1/2   **cup sugar**
2   **eggs**
1   **teaspoon vanilla extract, *McCormick*®**

INDOOR METHOD:
Preheat oven to
350 degrees F. Lightly
spray 13×9-inch baking
pan with nonstick
cooking spray; set aside.
Prepare bars as directed.
Bake for 40 to 45 minutes
or until bars just begin
to pull away from
sides of the pan. Cool
completely. Serve
as directed.

1. Set up grill for indirect cooking over medium heat (no heat source under bars; see page 19). Spray a 13×9-inch foil baking pan with nonstick cooking spray; set aside.

2. In a large mixing bowl, combine cake mix, butter, egg, and food coloring; beat with electric mixer on low speed until combined. Press cake mixture into prepared pan; set aside.

3. In a medium mixing bowl, beat cream cheese and sugar on medium speed until creamy. Add eggs and vanilla; beat until combined. Spread cream cheese mixture evenly over cake layer.

4. Place foil baking pan in a second foil baking pan for stability and insulation. Place on hot grill away from heat source. Cover grill and bake 40 to 50 minutes or until bars just begin to pull away from sides of the pan, rotating the pan halfway through cooking.

5. Remove from grill; cool completely. Cut into bars.

Lemon Cream Squares

servings 15 **prep time** 20 minutes
grilling time 40 minutes

YOU WILL NEED
Two 13×9-inch foil baking pans
Nonstick cooking spray
Large mixing bowl
Electric mixer
Medium mixing bowl

FOR LEMON LAYER:
1   box (18.25-ounce) lemon cake mix, *Betty Crocker*®
$^1/_2$ cup butter (1 stick), softened
1   egg

FOR LEMON CREAM LAYER:
16   ounces cream cheese, softened, *Philadelphia*®
$^1/_3$ cup sugar
1   box (3-ounce) lemon gelatin, *Jell-O*®
2   eggs

INDOOR METHOD:
Preheat oven to
350 degrees F. Lightly
spray 13×9 baking pan
with nonstick cooking
spray; set aside. Prepare
bars as directed. Bake for
40 to 45 minutes or until
bars just begin to pull
away from sides of the
pan. Cool completely.
Serve as directed.

1. Set up grill for indirect cooking over medium heat (no heat source under bars; see page 19). Spray 13×9-inch foil baking pan with nonstick cooking spray; set aside.

2. In a large mixing bowl, combine cake mix, butter, and egg. Beat with an electric mixer on low speed until combined. Press cake mixture evenly into prepared pan; set aside.

3. In a medium mixing bowl, beat cream cheese, sugar, and lemon gelatin on medium speed until creamy. Add eggs; beat until smooth. Spread cream cheese mixture evenly over cake layer.

4. Place foil baking pan in a second foil baking pan for stability and insulation. Place on hot grill away from heat source. Cover grill and bake 40 to 50 minutes or until bars just begin to pull away from sides of the pan, rotating pan halfway through cooking.

5. Remove from grill; cool completely. Cut into bars.

Ginger Peach Ice Cream Sandwiches

servings 8 prep time 25 minutes
grilling time 12 minutes
freezing time 1 hour; 10 minutes
standing time 10 minutes

YOU WILL NEED
Large bowl
2 foil sheet pans
Ice cream scoop

1	**package (17.5-ounce) sugar cookie mix,** *Betty Crocker*®
1/2	**cup butter (1 stick), melted**
1	**egg**
2	**tablespoons finely chopped crystallized ginger,** *McCormick*®
1	**teaspoon minced ginger,** *Christopher Ranch*®
3/4	**teaspoon ground ginger**
2	**pints peach ice cream,** *Häagen-Dazs*®

1. Set up grill for indirect cooking over medium heat (no heat source under cookies; see page 19).

INDOOR METHOD:
Preheat oven to 375 degrees F. Prepare cookies as directed, except drop onto an ungreased cookie sheet. Bake for 10 to 14 minutes. Cool for 1 minute on cookie sheet. Transfer to a wire rack and cool completely. Freeze cookies for at least 1 hour before completing step 4 as directed.

2. In a large bowl, combine all ingredients except the ice cream. Stir to form dough. Drop by rounded tablespoons onto ungreased foil sheet pan, forming at least 16 dough mounds. Place sheet pan on another foil sheet pan for stability and insulation.

3. Place foil sheet pan on grill away from heat. Cover grill; cook for 12 to 16 minutes or until golden brown. Remove from grill. Cool to room temperature. Freeze cookies for 1 hour.

4. Soften ice cream on the counter for 10 minutes prior to making cookie sandwiches. Place a scoop of ice cream on the flat side of one cookie. Sandwich with another cookie, flat side down. Carefully press together until ice cream reaches the edge of the cookies. Repeat with remaining cookies and ice cream. Freeze for 10 minutes. Serve cold.

Little Cowboy Cookies

makes 48 cookies prep time 10 minutes
baking time 7 minutes per batch

YOU WILL NEED
Large bowl
Cookie sheet

1	**package (17.5-ounce) sugar cookie mix,** *Betty Crocker*®
1/2	**cup butter (1 stick), melted**
1	**egg**
1	**cup oatmeal,** *Quaker*® *Oats*
3/4	**cup chopped walnuts,** *Blue Diamond*®
3/4	**cup peanut butter and milk chocolate morsels,** *Nestlé*® *Toll House*®

1. Preheat oven to 375 degrees F. In a large bowl, combine all ingredients. Stir until well combined.

2. Drop by rounded teaspoons onto ungreased cookie sheet. Bake for 7 to 9 minutes. Let stand on cookie sheet for 1 minute. Transfer to a wire rack; cool completely.

Cocktails

It's cocktail time! That's how I end every show on the Food Network, and it's guaranteed to get the conversation buzzing. Where there's fire, there has to be ice, tinkling in a glass with liquid libation. This chapter shakes it up with style, giving you all the ingredients for a fireside chat—liqueur-spiked beers, refreshing citrus coolers, red hot shots turbocharged with Tabasco®, and cool blue martinis that prove summer is a state of mind, easily summoned with a splash of fruit juice. It's a whole new attitude served on the rocks—for fun in the sun … or the snow.

The Recipes

Blueberry Sangria Lemonade

servings 4 **prep time** 5 minutes **chilling time** 1 hour

YOU WILL NEED
Large pitcher
Iced tea glasses

1½ **cups frozen blueberries, *Dole®***
1   **can (12-ounce) frozen pink lemonade concentrate, thawed, *Minute Maid®***
1   **bottle (750-ml) Chardonnay**
3   **cups lemon-lime soda, *Sprite®***
½   **cup cognac**
     Ice cubes (optional)

1. In a large pitcher, combine all ingredients (except the ice cubes) and stir. Refrigerate for 1 hour to allow flavors to blend.

2. Pour chilled mixture into iced tea glasses. Add ice cubes (optional).

Drunken Watermelon

servings 12 **prep time** 15 minutes

YOU WILL NEED
Melon baller
Large spoon
Blender
Strainer
Ladle
Glasses

1   **4-pound seedless watermelon**
2   **cups tequila**
1   **cup triple sec**
     Lemon-lime soda, *Sprite®*
     Ice cubes

1. With a knife, shave off the stem end of the watermelon (just enough so that it sits flat). Cut about 3 inches off the top of the watermelon. Using a melon baller, make melon balls out of about half of the watermelon; set aside.

2. Scoop out remaining watermelon with a large spoon. If desired, leave the rind intact to use as a punch bowl. In batches, transfer scooped-out melon (not the melon balls) to a blender and puree. Push watermelon puree through a strainer to remove pulp. Return pureed watermelon to watermelon-rind punch bowl or transfer to a large pitcher. Stir in tequila and triple sec. Top off with lemon-lime soda. To serve, ladle mixture into ice-filled glasses. Serve melon balls on the side.

Red Hot Shot

servings 1 **prep time** 5 minutes

YOU WILL NEED
Shot glass

¾   **shot pepper vodka, *Absolut®***
1   **splash of tomato juice**
1   **dash of hot pepper sauce, *Tabasco®***
     Ice cold beer

1. Fill a shot glass three-quarters with vodka. Add a splash of tomato juice and a dash of hot pepper sauce. Serve with ice cold beer as a chaser.

Paradise Punch

servings 6 **prep time** 5 minutes

YOU WILL NEED
Large pitcher
Iced tea glasses

½   **cup blanco tequila**
½   **cup vodka**
½   **cup light rum, *Bacardi®***
½   **cup gin**
2   **cups cranberry juice**
2   **cups pineapple juice**
     Ice cubes
     Pineapple wedges (optional)
     Small cocktail umbrellas (optional)

1. In a large pitcher, combine all ingredients (except pineapple wedges and cocktail umbrellas) and stir.

2. Pour mixture into iced tea glasses. Garnish with wedges of pineapple (optional) and small cocktail umbrellas (optional).

Cocojito

servings 1 **prep time** 5 minutes

YOU WILL NEED
Shot glass
Cocktail shaker
Highball glass, chilled

2 shots coconut rum, *Bacardi®*
5 fresh mint leaves, torn
1/2 shot cream of coconut, *Coco Lopez®*
1 splash of lime juice, *Rose's®*
Ice cubes
Club soda
Fresh mint sprig (optional)

1. Add coconut rum, mint leaves, cream of coconut, lime juice, and ice cubes to a cocktail shaker.

2. Shake several times and pour into chilled highball glass. Top with club soda. Garnish with a sprig of mint (optional).

Seaside Martini

servings 1 **prep time** 5 minutes

YOU WILL NEED
Cocktail shaker
Shot glass
Cocktail strainer
Martini glass

Ice cubes
2 shots light rum, *Bacardi®*
1/2 shot blue curaçao
2 shots pineapple juice
Pineapple slice (optional)

1. Fill a cocktail shaker with ice cubes. Add rum, blue curaçao, and pineapple juice.

2. Shake several times and strain into a martini glass. Garnish with a pineapple slice (optional).

Lakeside Cooler

servings 1 **prep time** 5 minutes

YOU WILL NEED
Cocktail shaker
Shot glass
Highball glass

Ice cubes
1 shot blanco tequila
1 shot vodka
1/2 shot blue curaçao
Tonic water

1. Fill a cocktail shaker with ice cubes. Add tequila, vodka, and blue curaçao.

2. Shake several times and pour into a highball glass. Top with tonic water.

Put the Lime in the Coconut

servings 1 **prep time** 5 minutes

YOU WILL NEED
Shot glass
Cocktail shaker
2 plates
Martini glass, chilled
Cocktail strainer

2 shots pineapple-coconut juice, *Kern's®*
1 splash lime juice, *Rose's®*
1 shot vanilla vodka, *Absolut®*
1/2 shot half-and-half
1/2 shot banana schnapps
Ice cubes
1/4 cup honey, *Sue Bee®*
1/4 cup coconut flakes, toasted, *Baker's®*
Lime slice (optional)

1. Add all ingredients (except honey, coconut, and lime slice) to a cocktail shaker.

2. Pour honey onto a plate. Place coconut on another plate. Dip the rim of chilled glass into honey; dip in coconut.

3. Shake the coconut juice mixture. To serve, carefully strain into chilled martini glass. Garnish with lime slice (optional).

Peach Martini

servings 1 **prep time** 5 minutes

YOU WILL NEED
Cocktail shaker
Shot glass
Cocktail strainer
Martini glass, chilled

    Ice cubes
1   shot peach vodka, *Absolut*®
1/2 shot peach schnapps
1/2 shot peach nectar, *Kern's*®
    Lemon-lime soda, *Sprite*®
    Fresh peach slice (optional)

1. Fill a cocktail shaker with ice cubes. Add vodka, schnapps, and nectar. Shake several times and strain into a martini glass.

2. Top off glass with lemon-lime soda. Garnish with a fresh peach slice (optional).

Passion Fruit Cooler

servings 6 **prep time** 5 minutes

YOU WILL NEED
Large pitcher
Highball glasses

1/2 cup passion fruit syrup, *Torani*®
1/2 cup peach nectar, *Kern's*®
1   liter orange-flavor seltzer water
1   cup light rum, *Bacardi*® (optional)
    Ice cubes

1. In a large pitcher, combine syrup, nectar, and seltzer water. Add rum (optional) and ice cubes. Stir well.

2. Pour into highball glasses.

Cowboy Cocktail

servings 1 **prep time** 5 minutes

YOU WILL NEED
Highball glass

3   fresh mint leaves
    Crushed ice
1/2 lime, juiced
1   bottle beer, *Corona*®
    Fresh mint sprig (optional)

1. Place mint leaves in bottom of highball glass. Fill with crushed ice.

2. Add lime juice and stir. Add beer. Garnish with a fresh mint sprig (optional).

Cowgirl Cooler

servings 12 **prep time** 10 minutes **standing time** 20 minutes

YOU WILL NEED
Saucepan
Colander
Large pitcher

1   2-inch piece fresh ginger, sliced
2   cups water
1   can (12-ounce) frozen lemonade concentrate, thawed, *Minute Maid*®
4 1/2 cups ginger ale, *Canada Dry*®
1 1/2 cups vodka
    Ice cubes
    Lemon slices (optional)

1. In a small saucepan, bring sliced ginger and water to a boil. Remove from heat and let stand for 20 minutes. Strain; reserve ginger water.

2. In a large pitcher, stir to combine thawed lemonade concentrate, ginger water, ginger ale, and vodka. Serve over ice. Garnish with lemon slices (optional).

Berry-tini

servings 1 **prep time** 5 minutes

YOU WILL NEED
Cocktail shaker
Cocktail strainer
Martini glass

    Ice cubes
2   **shots berry-flavor vodka**
1   **shot orange-flavor liqueur,** *Cointreau®*
1   **splash lime juice,** *Rose's®*
    Blueberry swizzle stick * (optional)

1. Fill a cocktail shaker with ice cubes. Add vodka, orange-flavor liqueur, and lime juice. Shake several times.

2. Strain into a martini glass. Garnish with blueberry swizzle stick (optional).

*TIP: To make blueberry swizzle stick, thread fresh blueberries onto a wooden or metal skewer.

Beer Ball Buffet

prep time 5 minutes

YOU WILL NEED
12-ounce beer mugs or glasses *
Shot glasses

1   **beer ball, pony keg, or 1.5-gallon mini keg of lager-style beer**
    Orange-flavor liqueur, *Grand Marnier®*
    Peach schnapps
    Coffee-flavor liqueur, *Kahlúa®*
    Passion fruit syrup, *Torani®*
    Tomato juice
    Hot pepper sauce, *Tabasco®*
    Worcestershire sauce
    Melon-flavor liqueur

1. Orange-Spiked Beer: Add 1 shot of orange-flavor liqueur to 12 ounces of beer.

2. Peach-Spiked Beer: Add 1 shot of peach schnapps to 12 ounces of beer.

3. Beer Buzz: Add 1 shot of coffee-flavor liqueur to 12 ounces of beer.

4. Beer Passion: Add 1 shot passion fruit syrup to 12 ounces of beer.

5. Red Eye: Add 1 shot of tomato juice to 12 ounces of beer.

6. Beer Mary: Add 1 shot of tomato juice, several drops of hot pepper sauce, and a splash of Worcestershire sauce to 12 ounces of beer.

7. South Wind: Add 1 shot of melon liqueur to beer.

*NOTE: 12 ounces equals 1 1/2 cups.

Index

Index (cont.)

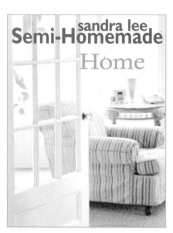

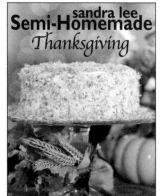

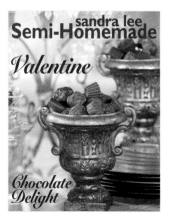

semihomemade.com

making life easier, better, and more enjoyable

Semihomemade.com has hundreds of ways to simplify your life—the easy Semi-Homemade way! You'll find fast ways to de-clutter, try your hand at clever crafts, create terrific tablescapes or decorate indoors and out to make your home and garden superb with style.

We're especially proud of our Semi-Homemakers club: a part of semihomemade.com which hosts other semihomemakers just like you. The club community shares ideas to make life easier, better, and more manageable with smart tips and hints allowing you time to do what you want! Sign-up and join today—it's free—and sign up your friends and family, too! It's easy the Semi-Homemade way! Visit the site today and start enjoying your busy life!

Sign yourself and your friends and family up to the semi-homemaker's club today!

tablescapes	home	garden	organizing	crafts
everyday & special days	cooking	entertaining	cocktail time	
Halloween	Thanksgiving	Christmas	Valentine's	Easter	New Year's

About Sandra Lee

Sandra Lee is a *New York Times* best-selling author and a nationally acclaimed lifestyle expert. Her signature Semi-Homemade approach to cooking, home decorating, gardening, crafting, entertaining, beauty, and fashion offers savvy shortcuts and down-to-earth secrets for creating a beautiful, affordable, and most importantly doable lifestyle.

Sandra Lee's cookbook series offers amazing meals in minutes, fabulous food fixin's, and sensational—yet simple—style ideas. *Semi-Homemade Cooking with Sandra Lee* is one of Food Network's hottest cooking shows, providing many helpful hints, timesaving techniques, tips, and tricks.

Find even more sensible, savvy solutions online at **semihomemade.com**.

Sandra Lee Semi-Homemade® Cookbook Series
Collect all these amazingly helpful, timesaving, and beautiful books!
Look for the series wherever quality books are sold.